AF477377

Frontis By 1963, when this picture was taken, the influence of the European Grand Prix cars was beginning to be felt, and the old Indianapolis roadster was on the way out. Here is one of Mickey Thompson's cars which Al Miller drove into ninth place. The car was designed to run on modern European type tyres, that is slicks, but was forced to use the Firestones seen in the picture.

Firestone
Thompson
Enterprises
Firestone
Mickey Thompson
84
84

PIT & PADDOCK

A BACKGROUND TO MOTOR RACING 1894-1978

Michael Frostick

Moorland Publishing

ISBN 0 86190 002 2

Typeset by Alacrity Phototypesetters,
Banwell Castle, Weston-super-Mare, Avon
and printed in Great Britain
by Redwood Burn Ltd, Trowbridge & Esher
for Moorland Publishing Co Ltd,
PO Box 2, Ashbourne, Derbyshire, DE6 1DZ

CONTENTS

ACKNOWLEDGEMENTS

The pictures in this book have come from a great variety of sources, and I am particularly indebted to Louis Klemantaski and the Library of the National Motor Museum at Beaulieu who have been by far the biggest contributors. I am also grateful to Dr Amari of the Museo Dell'Automobile Carlo Biscaretti de Ruffia at Turin, and the Fiat Centro Storico in the same city for their assistance. I must thank Dr Wiersch of the Volkswagen/Audi archives for much of the Auto Union information, as well as the press department at Daimler-Benz and those of many other companies. I should also like to give particular thanks to Griffith Borgesson for so much help with the identification of the Indianapolis cars, and to Michael Sedgwick and Nick Georgano for help with other obscure pictures.

A great number of books have obviously been consulted; but the following have been particularly helpful: *The Grand Prix Car* (Volumes 1 & 2) by Laurence Pomeroy, *Power and Glory* by William Court, *Record of Motor Racing* by Gerald Rose, *The Encyclopedia of Motor Sport* edited by G. N. Georgano, and William Boddy's famous *History of Brooklands Motor Course*.

INTRODUCTION

At the first meeting between author and publisher to discuss this book they had in mind a volume dedicated to the building of racing cars, but they shared considerable doubts and misgivings as to the practicality of their notion. The building of racing cars is, and always has been, a very secret business and the buildings where the work takes place are out of bounds to most of the world, photographers in particular being *persona non grata*. For all that, it was decided that approaches should be made and archives searched, to see if such a venture was possible. Alas, in the event, the worst of their joint forebodings proved all too true, but, as usual, the cloud of disappointment had a silver lining. Among the many pictures that came to light during the search were a great number depicting cars and personalities, taken long after the cars had been made, but usually before they were raced, and they were offered on the 'Is this the kind of thing you're after?', basis. Their theme was so persistent that, if they proved one book impossible, they made it all too clear in which direction the alternative lay.

And so to *Pit and Paddock* and a new set of problems, the chief of which, as with so many motoring books, was simply what to leave out. Since so much must be missed, agonising decisions have to be taken and the first was to omit very largely the most recent years, since these are more easily remembered, and many of the more interesting photographs have already appeared in magazines and books. Outside that obvious limit, we have concentrated on the earliest days, and the present, to show how little the business of racing cars has changed. There are excursions into the Grands Prix of the Hitler era, of Le Mans in the immediate post war years when its popularity reached an all time high; and some special note of those two great man-made circuits, Brooklands and Indianapolis.

In the end it has to be a thumb-nail sketch rather than a full portrait, but the essential character is there, together with the changeless struggle of man and machine to do better than the other fellow.

One last word: throughout the book we have refrained from putting obvious notes asking the reader to compare the later pictures with the earlier, for example groups of mechanics behind the cars they have built, scenes in the pits, team managers talking with their drivers. The comparisons are usually obvious, often rewarding, and in the most astonishing way literally illustrate the truth of the French proverb 'Plus ça change, plus c'est la même chose'. We hope, therefore, that having browsed through this book, the reader will indulge in a little turning to and fro, in order to give the kaleidoscope of history a better chance to unfold.

1 THE EARLY DAYS

Race you round the houses — race you to Bordeaux

The first recorded motoring event was scheduled to be held in the suburbs of Paris in 1887, two or three years after the motor car had been put into production by Benz and Daimler. Unhappily when the time came for the start only one car turned up, so there was no event and history has turned our attention to what is now generally regarded as the first motor race, (although it was not really a race at all), the Paris to Rouen Trial of 1894, sponsored by a French newspaper. When entries closed in April of that year there were no less than a hundred and two of them. Many of these were no more than pipe dreams, just how many can be judged from the fact that when the competitors lined up for the start, in the Boulevard Maillot, there were only twenty-one.

Looking back, nearly a century later, one realises how little the motor racing scene has changed. True, the cars may have developed beyond all recognition, the public interest may have grown out of all proportion, (though one could doubt this), but the men remain very much as they were, and the organisers just as unpopular as ever. Although all kinds of weird devices were entered for this first event, when it came to the start, all were either steam or petrol driven. They were given twelve hours to make the journey of about eighty miles from Paris to Rouen and the first vehicle home was the De Dion steam tractor which made it in six hours and forty-eight minutes. It did *not* get first prize, because, after the usual disagreement, it was disqualified as it had needed two men to look after it. However, it was awarded second prize, the first being considered a tie between a Peugeot and a Panhard which had actually come second and third. One learns, at least, that if some of the present decisions by race organisers seem a little strange, then they have ample precedent.

Following hard on the heels of this first event, enthusiasts soon got together and, finding that no newspaper would back a further race, they formed the Automobile Club of France and did the job themselves. The next event was a race from Paris to Bordeaux and back, after which inter-city races became all the rage, until the ill-fated Paris-Madrid of 1903. It is said that on this occasion some three million people lined the course which was an ordinary main road, and as spectator control was almost non-existent, men, women and children, not to mention horses and dogs, pigs and cattle, and chickens, were all over the road. There were clouds of dust behind each car, dangerously masking the arrival of the next. Before the race reached Bordeaux there were more than twelve dead and goodness knows how many injured, so that the French Government stopped the race, even demanding that the cars be towed to the railway station by horses, before being shipped back to Paris by train. That was the end of town-to-town races on public roads, but it was the beginning of circuit races as we know them, and not far from the building of special race tracks, like Brooklands and Indianapolis, where spectators could be controlled, and where money could be charged at the gate. Lung cancer and smoking, television and advertising were not yet known as forces which would bring about the commercial sponsorship we endure today, and the motor cars were entered by their makers for the publicity it would give them in their ordinary sales to the public. Even so for the men who actually built the cars, for the men who drove them, and for the mechanics who at that time rode with them, the pressures and excitements were essentially as they are now; and the devotion to fine workmanship and good design were as important then as at any time since. It is a scene which has changed completely, and yet is the same as ever, and the pictures on the ensuing pages make this amply clear.

However, the problems were different even if of the same magnitude, for in motor racing then, as now, there are no its and buts, either you win or you do not, and however good and sensible your car, and however brave and daring your driver, there is an element of luck which is the saving grace of the game, for the best man does not always win.

Roads at that time would be described today as cart tracks, for there was no tar on the surfaces, though most of them were laid on the principles of J.L. McAdam, who had died in 1836, where successive layers of broken stone of approximately equal size were rolled on top of each other. Racing cars skidding round corners soon broke up this surface, and the road became rutted like a modern forest stage in a rally, indeed that is probably the best comparison one could make. Tyres unfortunately were not the present day steel-belted radials, but thin, narrow, rubber rings of uncertain strength and short life. Regulations in those days more often than not demanded that the only people who could work on a car during the race were the driver and his mechanic, (who travelled alongside him), so that they needed many skills not demanded of the modern Grand Prix man.

They were under perpetual attack from flying stones and dust, so that if their appearance in goggles, gauntlets, face masks and thick coats seems odd, it was very necessary. Many of the races were long and great physical stamina was needed, especially as frequent tyre changes would add to the burden. Dedication was as much in demand in 1900 as seventy years later. To get into the game then was no easier than now, indeed perhaps more difficult, since there was less game to get into. Money helped, as ever, and there were many wealthy amateurs. Works drivers were soon on the scene, but these were largely recruited from among the company mechanics of the major manufacturers. Men like Lancia and Nazzaro came up that way, as indeed did Enzo Ferrari himself, many years later.

There was a strong flavour of national pride in all the events once they had moved out of France, and into Europe generally. The most entertaining being the Gordon Bennet races, the cup having been given by an expatriate American newspaper proprietor, who had incidentally also been responsible for sending Stanley to Africa to find Livingstone. The rules called for a race not so much between drivers or even manufacturers, as between teams of three cars nominated by a recognised club. The cars had wholly to be made in their country of origin, which led to all sorts of complaints, for example, 'Was the leather on the seats of the German cars made from the skins of German cows?' There was no end to it. In addition there was great snobbery about drivers and some very capable men had to be left out in favour of others whose only claim to fame was that they were Masters of Fox Hounds, and so it went on. Eventually everyone, particularly the French, became very tired of the whole business, and they started the French Grand Prix, from which all modern racing springs.

There were formulae governing racing from the beginning, weight being the earliest limit, and some strange ideas followed, which produced among other things huge single-cylinder engines half as high as a man.

The earliest formula was introduced in 1902 and was a limit of weight of 1,000 kilogrammes, which is why in many of the early pictures cars are seen at the weigh-in, which was in fact the scrutineering that we know today. Eventually a special committee of the members of the recognised Automobile Clubs, (the AIACR), drew up the rules for Grand Prix racing, and although the formula changed many times over the years the predominent size seems to have been the 3-litre engine we have today.

The Americans had their share of road racing, and the Vanderbilt Cup events were in many respects the equivalent of the Gordon Bennet races in Europe. Indianapolis was built in 1909 and the first of the famous '500's was on 30 May 1911. From the very start there was a good deal of transatlantic movement to take part in races, many Europeans going to Indianapolis well before World War I, and equally Americans participating in European events. For example Goux in a Peugeot and Thomas in a Delage had both won Indianapolis before the war, and when the French Grand Prix was revived in 1921 Murphy won it in a Duesenberg.

Star drivers were well established by the turn of the century, the most glamorous was perhaps the mysterious Hungarian, who won the first French Grand Prix for Renault and delighted in the name of Szisz, which, if you understand such things, you will pronounce 'Sheesh'. The last years before World War I also saw the foundation of the great engine developments carried out by Peugeot, to Henry's designs, who was in turn supported both on the circuit and in the drawing office by the team drivers Boillot, Goux and Zucarelli. The cars had, for the first time, 16-valve, four-cylinder engines with twin overhead camshafts and were the true forerunners of today's Grand Prix machinery. So we find a young man in 1910, passionately interested in motor racing, having the same concerns regarding both men and machines as his great-grandson has today.

---

1   The first racing car, or more accurately the first car that Mercedes raced. In those far off days, of course, Mercedes meant Daimler, for it was Emil Jellinek who had decided to take over the business of selling Daimlers in Europe, on the understanding that they were named after his daughter Mercedes. He also demanded that William Maybach, the company's chief designer, should make a high performance car. This is the car, the 35hp, 5·9-litre model, (you needed a large engine to get 35hp in those days), which made its first appearance as a Mercedes racing car in the 1901 Pau Grand Prix driven by Lorraine Barrow. It was not so much its appearance in a race, but rather its specification which makes everyone regard it as the father of all racing cars. Not unusual now, it had many outstanding features for its day such as a pressed steel frame, a honeycomb radiator, mechanically operated inlet valves, and a gate-change for the gearbox. All these things moved it away from the horseless carriage and into the realms of real motoring.

2   The Paris-Vienna race of 1902 was almost the end of the inter-city races and even then the race, which went through Switzerland, was neutralised through that territory as the Swiss would not have racing on public roads. This is Valentin driving an Ader to the weigh-in. Ader, who was a telephone engineer, was a leading exponent of the 'V' engine. He made V-twins and V4s and then by putting two V4s together made a V8. This example is the V-twin of 1,556cc: two were entered for the race, and one finished.

1

2

3   Renault number 18, driven by Louis Renault, whose brother in a similar car, number 147, won the event. This was a triumph for the light over the heavy vehicles and an early success for Renault. This car finished thirteenth. Marcel Renault was one of those who died in one of the many accidents in the Paris-Madrid the following year.

4   And so to the ill-fated 1903 Paris-Madrid, that got no further than Bordeaux. It may have been helpful to have so many spectators around to give a hand when needed, as with Civelli de Bosch, shown here with his Clement, which did not reach Bordeaux; but on the whole there were too many people with no idea of the dangers to which they were exposed. This was an occasion when having a car that broke down might have been good luck, and not bad, for at least you lived to race another day.

5 British hopes and interests were largely concentrated on the Napier entered by Mark Mayhew, seen here at the weigh-in. Napier had had two very successful years in 1901 and 1902, but by 1903 their star was on the wane, and only the Mayhew car turned out for the Paris-Madrid, and did not get to Bordeaux. However oddly dressed it was necessary to be on race day, there was still a great air of respectability on the days prior to the race, with suits for both driver and mechanic, though the latter's cloth cap, in acknowledgement of his position, would give today's social observer something to talk about. The car is a 35-hp model and the actual machine, together with the 1902 Gordon Bennett model, eventually found a home in America, where both were restored to their original pristine condition.

6 Looking a good deal more chauffeur-like is M. Baras, also seen taking his Darracq to the weigh-in. He did better than some other drivers, managing to be the fifth to arrive at Bordeaux, and also to get second place in the light car class. The total absence of coachwork other than seats to sit on, was a feature of racing cars at that time which has found an echo in recent years. Unnecessary weight is after all unnecessary weight, and the view of what was going on on the road ahead was little short of phenomenal.

7 Ettore Bugatti ran into trouble with this De Dietrich that he had designed especially for this event. Long before he set up on his own, indeed before he was even twenty-one, Bugatti had entered into a contract with Baron de Dietrich to design cars for him. They were called De Dietrich-Bugatti's, and enjoyed considerable competition success sometimes driven by Bugatti himself. On this occasion, however, fate seems to have been against him, for the car, built specially for the Paris-Madrid event, was refused entry because there was insufficient visibility for the driver. That takes some believing when looking at the photograph today, but the trouble seems to have been that the seat was too far back, and that the bonnet obscured part of the road immediately ahead of the car. A close look at most of the other contenders shows that in this particular respect they were probably better. At all events the Bugatti was a non-starter.

8 A happier moment for Baron de Dietrich was the start of the Circuit des Ardennes, in Belgium, in 1903. Here De Brou, seen at the start, managed third place. The cars were started separately which is why there is no Grand Prix line up. Enthusiastic historians will be interested to note that in those days Michelin sold oil as well as tyres, and that the publicity value of motor racing was already appreciated.

9 The Ardennes race was won by Baron de Crawhez in a Panhard, seen here about to go onto the weighbridge before the race began. It was not a steam car, so there seems no proper explanation for the jet of steaming water that is being ejected from the near side, nor of the two curious packages on the bonnet. The mechanic on many of the earlier cars sat lower than the driver and frequently with his feet over the side rather than under the bonnet. This picture gives a good idea of such a seat, but one hopes that the moor man kept his feet out of the hot water.

MICHELIN

10 Another important race in 1903 was the Gordon Bennett race held in Ireland. As the previous event had been won by an Englishman, it fell to England to have the honour to organise the next one, which would have been fine if the law had not expressly forbidden it. The result was that it had to be held in Ireland which, for the purposes of argument at least, could rank as part of the British Isles. This was well before the troubles which led to Ireland becoming a separate state. Cars, of course, came from all over the world, including this unusual-looking Winton from America. Already the brighter motor engineers had realised that by reducing the frontal area one was gaining speed, even if the driver had to be left perched up in the air. Winton was one of the first builders of production cars in America and took a deep interest in racing. For this event he produced two cars both with horizontal engines, in-line affairs with their cylinder heads to the right. This is the smaller of the two cars, driven by Percy Owen, seen getting ready to go to the start. It has a four-cylinder engine of 8·5 litres capacity. In the event neither car finished.

11 By this time the big names were beginning to make themselves felt and here is a 1903-4 Mercedes racing car, a four-cylinder 90-hp model, with some of the Mercedes team standing behind it. Second from the left is Jenatzy, famous as the first man to cover a mile in a minute, in his electric car, and fourth from the left is Baron de Caters, another team driver. While it cannot be said that a title was absolutely necessary before you were allowed to drive, it obviously helped, as some of the preceding pictures make all too clear.

12 It was becoming clear that design was beginning to crystalize, for here is the 60-hp Fiat of 1904, tipo Corsa, which shows a remarkable similarity to the Mercedes above, though why it was given four seats is something of a mystery.

11

12

13   The French Grand Prix was the father of all
Grands Prix and was first held in 1906, though the
French had already been talking about it for two
years. It came about because everyone, but especially
the French, were tired of the Gordon Bennett races.
This was mainly because only one team was permitted from each country, and there were already a
mass of manufacturers more than ready to compete in
an international event which would show off their
wares. The French Grand Prix therefore became a
race for manufacturers rather than nations and as
such it was doomed to success. It took place at
Le Mans, but not on the circuit we know today,
rather on an immense triangle with a sixty-four-mile
lap. Thirty-two cars started, representing three countries, and thirteen makes, of which no less than ten
were French. Szisz won the race for Renault.

14   Among the competitors was Civelli de Bosch,
this time driving a Gregoire and is seen here going
into the paddock for the weigh-in. There was a
maximum weight limit of 1,007 kilogrammes.

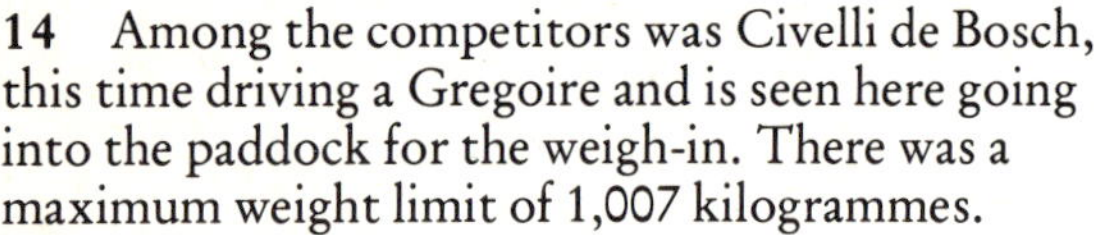

15   Here is young Clement, whose father built the
Clement Bayard which he was driving, actually on the
weigh-bridge before the start. Despite a somewhat
unlucky-looking number he came third. The obser-
vant will note the early cine-camera on the left.

16   This is Jenatzy's Mercedes in the pits. Jenatzy
was past his prime by now, and had further to suffer
from an eye injury in this race. Perhaps the most
interesting thing in the picture is the idea it gives of
the kind of road people raced over in those days. In
fact part of the circuit on this occasion was so bad
that a temporary plank road was laid over it, but they
went on racing just the same.

17   An Itala photographed in 1906 at Longchamps,
outside Paris. The driver is probably Itala's leading
man Cagno; one has to say probably as the picture
has no caption and the prevalence of chauffeurs' hats
and moustaches makes absolute identification uncertain. We know the picture was taken soon after
Itala had scored the second fastest time in the speed
trials at Dourdon, and about that time Itala, with
Cagno as driver, had been doing very well. They won
the 1905 Coppa Florio and Cagno won the 1906
Targa Florio with Italas also in second, fourth and
fifth places. Itala also had a lot of publicity from
other efforts on the open road. A Mr H. R. Pope, for
example, drove one from Monte Carlo to London at
an average speed of 31 mph. And, of course, it was an
Itala which, in the hands of Prince Scipione Borghese,
won the famous Peking to Paris race.

18 Back to the French Grand Prix, this time 1907, and the Fiat F1 130-hp model in the pits. Improvements had been made to the surface by more planks, which were at least easier to work on than the rough road, where every dropped spanner was immediately covered in dust. The interest here is in the driver, with one hand still on the wheel, for he is none other than Vincenzo Lancia, before he became a motor manufacturer, and while he was still one of the best known of Fiat's works drivers. His mechanic (with back to the camera), is P. Bordino, but there is no information on the Peter Ustinov-like character on the right with the red-cross armband!

19 Although we are concerned with men rather than machines, the racing cars of this period were such magnificent monsters that one needs to look at them in some detail to see what the drivers and mechanics were up against. 1907 was Fiat's great year. There were three really important races, the Targa Florio, the Kaiserpreis and the French Grand Prix, and Fiat won them all. It was not as easy as all that, either, for it was before there was an established international Formula, and the rules for all three races were different. In the Targa Florio the bore was restricted, in the German race there were limits on both engine size and weight, and when it came to the French Grand Prix the organizers thought engines were getting too big, (and they were right), so they introduced a fuel consumption rule of 30 litres per 100 kilometres, to try to get smaller engines. Fiat's answer to the last of the three problems was the F2 pictured here. The chassis, without the body, weighed 2,260 pounds, had a wheelbase of 112·2 inches and a track of 58·17 inches. With it Felice Nazzaro, who had already won the two previous races, swept to victory at Dieppe, beating Szisz in the Renault, who had won the previous French Grand Prix at Le Mans.

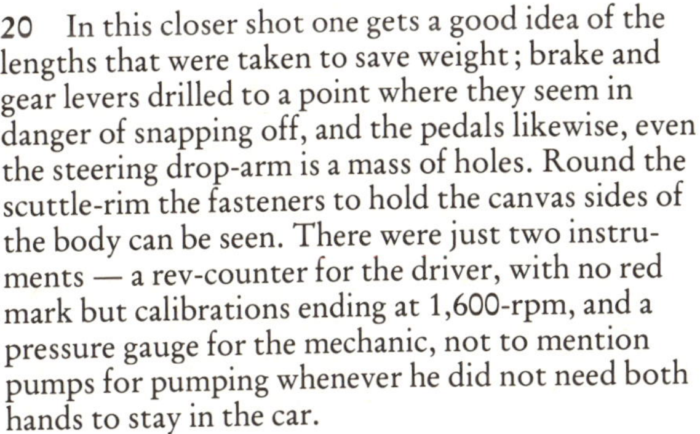

19

20

21

20   In this closer shot one gets a good idea of the lengths that were taken to save weight; brake and gear levers drilled to a point where they seem in danger of snapping off, and the pedals likewise, even the steering drop-arm is a mass of holes. Round the scuttle-rim the fasteners to hold the canvas sides of the body can be seen. There were just two instruments — a rev-counter for the driver, with no red mark but calibrations ending at 1,600-rpm, and a pressure gauge for the mechanic, not to mention pumps for pumping whenever he did not need both hands to stay in the car.

21   The inlet side of the 16,286cc engine. The huge exposed rockers were drilled like everything else and the low tension magneto can be seen driven by gears from the front of the crankshaft. The odd placing of the spark plugs makes one wonder about the internal shape of the cylinder head. Both inlet and exhaust valves were operated by one push rod, there being in effect two rocker arms working inside each other.

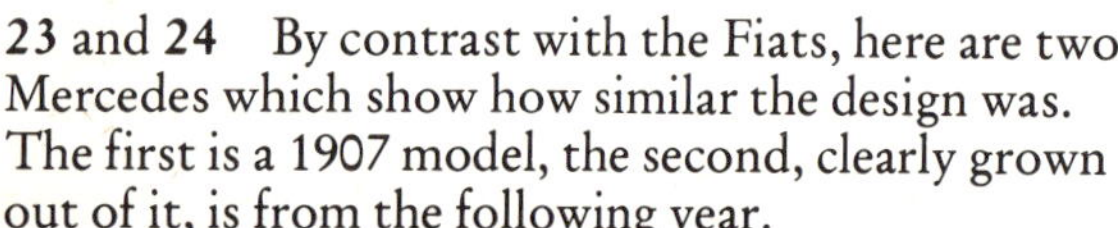

22

22 Another of Fiat's famous works drivers, Wagner, seen here with his mechanic, Ferro, in a similar car. The picture was taken at Savannah, Georgia, presumably just before Wagner won the Grand Prix there in 1907.

23 and **24** By contrast with the Fiats, here are two Mercedes which show how similar the design was. The first is a 1907 model, the second, clearly grown out of it, is from the following year.

24

25 Back to Fiat again for the S61 of 1908. This was built principally for the 1909 French Grand Prix. It is most notable for its use of an overhead camshaft, and four valves per cylinder. The car shown in this picture is one of the third version models as prepared for racing.

26 With the mechanics, after winning the Giro Emilia in 1908, Felice Nazzaro is standing in front of his Fiat, hand in pocket. Nazzaro was one of the truly great drivers. He started his career as an apprentice with Fiat and quickly became one of their most prized drivers. His ability to get on with difficult customers led him to become Vincenzo Florio's chauffeur, (Florio founded the Targa Florio in Sicily), and in that capacity he went on driving in races. Like Lancia, he eventually began building cars himself but he did not have Lancia's success, and sold his business interests in 1916. He went back to Fiat and went on racing until 1924 when he became head of Fiat's competition department. He died in 1940.

27

28

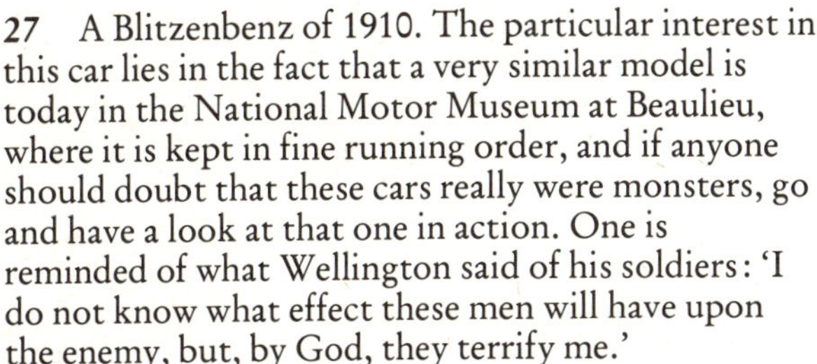

27 A Blitzenbenz of 1910. The particular interest in this car lies in the fact that a very similar model is today in the National Motor Museum at Beaulieu, where it is kept in fine running order, and if anyone should doubt that these cars really were monsters, go and have a look at that one in action. One is reminded of what Wellington said of his soldiers: 'I do not know what effect these men will have upon the enemy, but, by God, they terrify me.'

28 Alissandro Cagno again in a 1908 Itala. The demands of press photographers and publicity men were no less in those far off days, or so it seems. Bonnet straps undone, and a flat rear tyre make the hastiness of the picture more than a little obvious.

29 Vincenzo Lancia seen here for the first time in one of his own cars, having won the Targa d'Oro, (the gold plate), of the Modena Automobile Association.

30 One of the famous S74 Fiats, similar to those which did so well in America, but seen here, unusually, with wire wheels in the version prepared for private customers and road use.

31 Here is the same car with its more usual wooden wheels, as raced in America.

32 As has all too often been the case, it was
Germany and Italy who were making the running at
this moment. There had been a temporary abandon-
ment of racing in Europe in 1909 and most of the
competitors had crossed the Atlantic to continue
over there, Benz among them. The Germans had not
done too well during the ensuing year or two, but late
in 1912 they came up with the Blitzenbenz, a huge
monster with a 21,504cc engine, said to give over
200hp. V. Hemery finally got it up to 125·95mph at
Brooklands in November 1909 and then, in America,
Barney Oldfield got it up to 131·724mph and thereby
claimed the World Land Speed Record. He subsequently drove the car widely on American tracks
and became a national hero with it, (and indeed without it). The car is now in the Mercedes museum at
Stuttgart.

33 Not to be outdone by the Germans the Fiat
company made this car, the S76. Certainly of all the
monsters at that time this was the greatest monster
of them all. The car was fitted with an airship power
unit, a four-cylinder, twin-block unit of 190 × 125mm
giving no less than 28,353 litres, said to produce
290bhp at 1,900rpm. It is seen here, in 1911, outside
the Fiat works and time has erased any knowledge of
the identity of the various men sitting in it, or
standing behind, though the driver looks like
Nazarro.

34 The front view of the S76 which gives the lie to the story that you had to stand on the dumb-irons to fill the radiator, though indeed the radiator cap was more than 5ft from the road. This picture illustrates how slim the car was, and how little the occupants were actually within its body. The starting handle is interesting and can only have been for turning the engine over, no one could have cranked it; it was, in fact, started by compressed air from a built-in system.

35 This is the engine of the S76 in the Fiat aviation department, with Alessandro Cagno standing to the left of the picture. Cagno, who had been one of Fiat's top drivers, moved over to the aviation section in 1908; he made a comeback to racing in 1923. He was living quietly in retirement in Turin as recently as 1970.

36

37

36 So far the British do not appear to have had much success, although they had done well in many events. Perhaps they were more shy of the photographers than the precocious Continentals. Anyway here, in the Coupe de L'Auto races at Dieppe, is Hancock's Vauxhall in the pits, not during the race but before the start, fitting wet-weather tyres, (which in those days would have been exactly the same as dry weather ones).

37 Alfa now made their debut, (Signor Romeo had not yet taken an interest in the firm), and this car is the 24hp Spider. The 24hp in its various forms was the first car they made. At the wheel is Signor Stracca, one of the company testers, and beside him, Cav Agostoni, the works manager.

38 Meanwhile the monster Fiats were doing very well. Not only had they gone to America, they had come back with some American drivers. Here is David Bruce Brown reversing into his bay in the paddock, not it would seem without dust and heat, on the occasion of the 1912 French Grand Prix. After winning the 1910 American Great Prize in a Benz, he joined Fiat in 1911 and did very well indeed. He was in Europe for the 1912 French Grand Prix driving with Wagner, and another American Ralph De Palma, in the team. He won the first day's event, but on the second day of the two-day race he had trouble with his petrol pipe and was disqualified for taking on fuel in the wrong place. He went on to finish third although in fact disqualified. This was the race in which the Grand Prix Peugeots with their twin-overhead camshaft engines, first appeared.

39 This is Ralph De Pala in the pits. Helping hands could hold a tyre on the pit counter, but only the driver and the mechanic were allowed to work on the car.

40 A flashback to America with the same model (Fiat S74) in the paddock before the 1912 Santa Monica race. Car number 44 was driven by Teddy Tetzlaff, known as Terrible Teddy and seen on the left. The huge churns were used for petrol, which was put into the car with the outsize funnel seen in the foreground.

41 and **42**   After the Peugeot breakthrough in the 1912 French Grand Prix with their revolutionary twin-overhead camshaft engine, several manufacturers tried technical innovations. Among the more interesting were the three Italas entered for the 1913 French Grand Prix. These, the largest-engined cars in the race, had rotary valves and a capacity of 7,853cc. A strike in the Turin works had meant that they had had to do a great many tests at Brooklands. They were driven by Nazarro, making a return to racing, with Moriondo and H. R. Pope making up the team. In these pictures the car is driven by Guido Bigio, the company's deputy administrator, with his mechanic Ardizzone. The strange marks on the bonnet, behind the radiator, are not photographic mishaps but are on the car. The vertical petrol tank, which was for test only, is interesting and so is the exhaust which used a ram effect. The poor mechanic took the full blast from the enormous exhaust pipe.

41

42

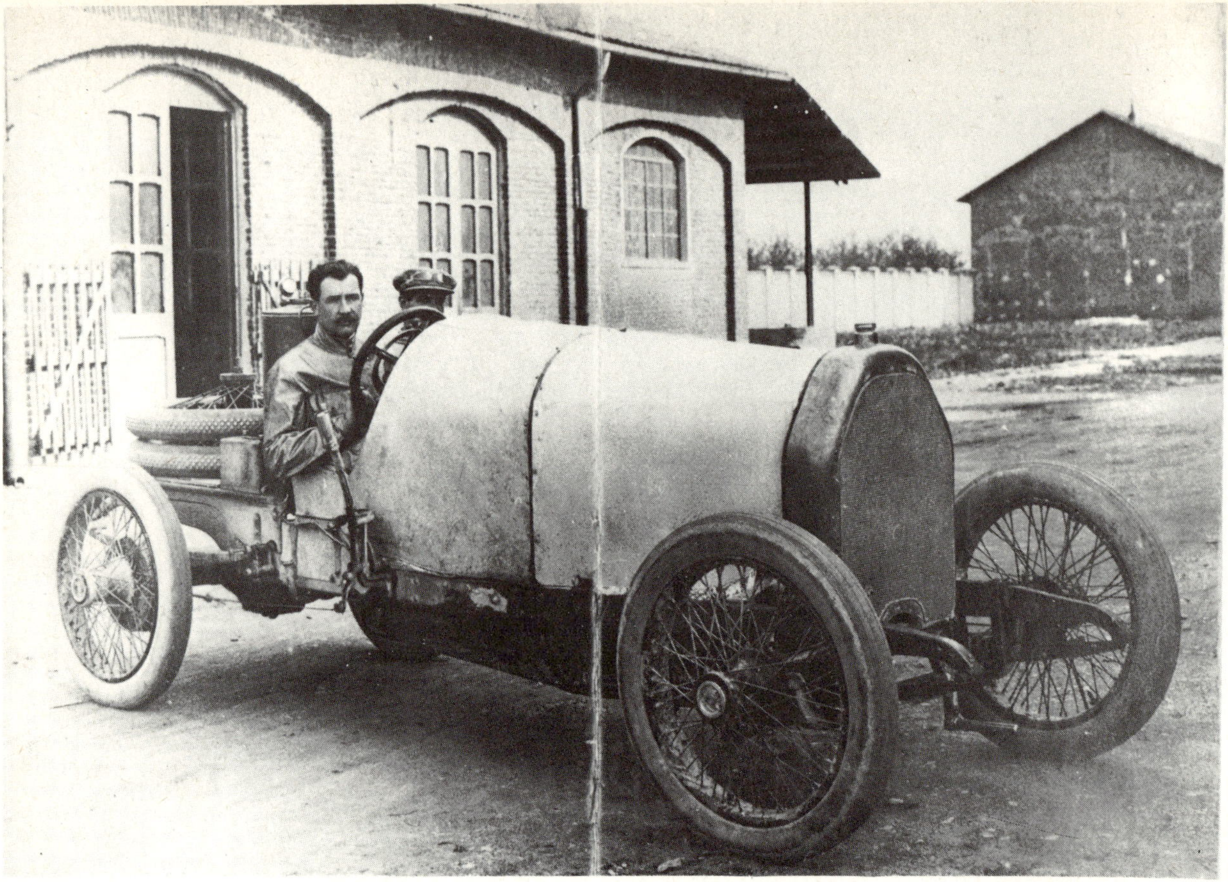

43

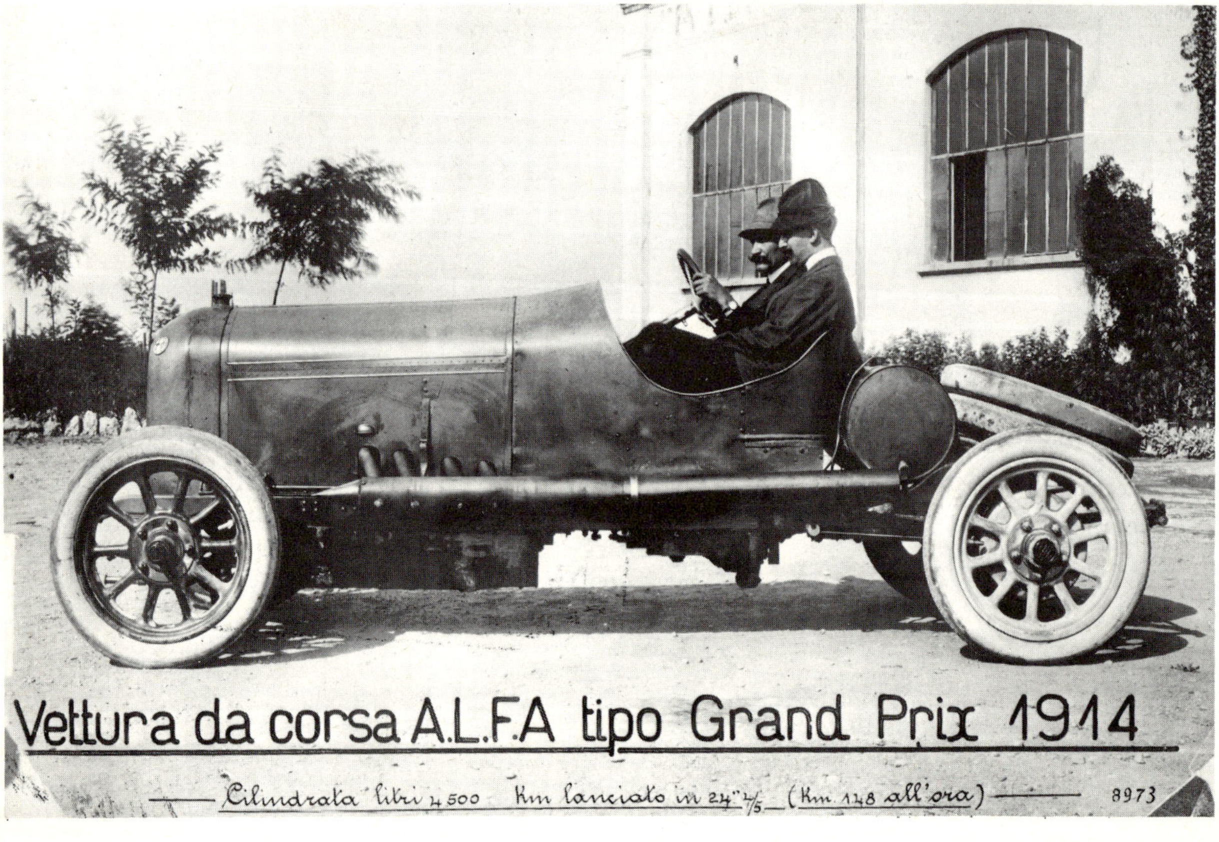

44

Cilindrata litri 4500 Km lanciato in 24" 2/5 (Km 148 all'ora) 8973

43 The great Nazzaro himself, also on test, or at least while the cars were. In the race they were painted a darker colour and had the conventional bolster fuel talk, with the spare wheels canted at an angle to accommodate it.

44 To bridge the gap between the time before and the time after World War I, here is the 1914 Grand Prix Alfa, which did not in fact race until well after the war in a much modified form. At the wheel is its designer Merosi.

45 Merosi is also seen here with something of a curiosity. It is probably a compressor, for he did later design a very successful commercial unit. The Alfa caption has great charm: it simply says, 'Merosi with . . .'

46 Merosi again, in 1953 when he was eighty-one. He was one of the great figures at the beginning of the Italian automobile industry. Designers, unlike racing drivers, let their praises go unsung, to which this small tribute offers some redress.

2 THE MAN-MADE CIRCUITS

Brooklands and The Brickyard

Once the tragedy of the Paris-Madrid race had driven motor racing off the open roads, there were but two alternatives. First, and for very many years foremost, was the idea of closing a circuit of public roads on which to hold the race. This was done widely in Europe, and not at all in Britain, for legal, rather than any other, reasons. The British road circuit races were all held in Northern Ireland or the Isle of Man, where it was possible to get government permission. The second, which is what concerns us, was the building of special circuits on which motor racing could take place. The most famous of these were probably Brooklands, at Weybridge, just outside London, and Indianapolis, just outside the American city of that name. there were others, of course, of almost equal importance, such as Montlhery in France, Monza in Italy, and the Avus circuit near Berlin. There were also some others which never became established, such as the circuit at Miramas in the south of France which was only used for a very few years. In America there were literally hundreds of board tracks and other small circuits, but there need be no apologies for taking Brooklands and Indianapolis as representative of the two sides of the Atlantic.

Brooklands was built by private enterprise, as indeed was Indianapolis, the former in 1906 and the latter in 1909. The existence of Brooklands, which was the world's first real Motor Course, was due solely to H. F. Locke King, who built it on his estate at Weybridge entirely at his own expense. Apart from racing one of the principal provisions the owner wished to make was for the testing of cars, since the universal speed limit of 20mph, and the enthusiasm of the police, rendered this hazardous if not impossible on the ordinary roads. The course took a year to build and was first opened to the public in the summer of 1907. The track was actually designed by a Colonel Holden of the Royal Engineers, and was something of a *tour de force* in engineering terms, part of the steep Member's Banking, for example, having to be taken over the River Wey.

The regulations for the first motor car meeting to be held there now seem more than a little comic, since the whole thing was done on Jockey Club lines — hence the finishing straight incorporated in the track. Originally the cars did not even have numbers, but their drivers wore coloured 'silks' as do jockeys, and the events were started by Hugh Owen who had been a starter for the Jockey Club. If the truth be told, racing got off to a rather shaky start, with lawsuits from the local residents about noise, and an unfortunate death. The facilities provided by the clubhouse however were considerable and as well as the Brooklands Automobile Racing Club, (the famous BARC), there was soon to be a flying club as well, and the place became a real mecca for enthusiasts, who were mostly rich, and upper-middle if not upper-upper class. 'The right crowd and no crowding' was an advertised slogan, and there was very little of the 'chips with everything' attitude that characterises many racing circuits today.

Almost from the start a great majority of Brooklands races were handicap events, which enabled all and sundry to compete against all and sundry, and a side-valve Morgan to have (theoretically) as good a chance as a supercharged Bentley. This was largely due to the skill of the handicappers and of the timekeeper, A. V. Ebblewhite, known to everyone as 'Ebby', his small stout figure in a dark suit, whatever the weather, who was as much part of Brooklands as the concrete itself. As might be expected, on non-racing days the place abounded with engineers of great fame testing their ideas; but due to the need for cars to be fitted with 'Brooklands silencers' before they raced, the track remained outside the Grand Prix scene. These Grands Prix became more important as the thirties wore on, so Brooklands's place in the motoring world was diminished, if not in the eyes of British enthusiasts then at least in the eyes of the world. There had been some great and important races at the track, the annual '500' for example, almost vying with Indianapolis; but when World War II came, and the aircraft people moved back, the place was sold up, largely, as far as one can make out, due to the financial actions of Sir Malcolm Campbell, who, one would have assumed, should have known better.

On the other side of the Atlantic the circuit at Indianapolis had very similar beginnings in that it was built by private enterprise, but not by one man. Credit for the idea goes to Carl G. Fisher who decided, when no-one else appeared to be interested, to do the job himself. He got financial help from two other Indianapolis business men, Arthur C. Newby and Frank H. Wheeler. Like Brooklands, it got off to an uncertain start. The circuit was due to open on 4 July 1909 but as it was unfinished, that had to be put off until 19 August, but even before the day's racing was over the track had begun to disintegrate. This does not seem to have daunted the owners, for they closed the circuit down, and in the space of sixty-three days, had the whole track resurfaced with 3,200,000 ordinary paving bricks, at a cost of $155,000. Consequently it was henceforth known as 'The Brickyard'. The paving bricks, but not the name, have now, of course, gone. By 1911 the owners and organisers had decided that too much racing was unprofitable, and the right thing to do would be to concentrate their efforts on one big event a year scheduled to take place at the end of May. All sorts of ideas were considered, of up to 1,000 miles, and 24 hours; but in the end they decided on a 500-mile race since the whole event could then take place in daylight.

The story of the '500' is more than well documented. At the beginning of its life, as in more recent years, there had been a lot of European interest and European success, but in its middle period the interest and success was almost a hundred per cent American. Out of this and the things associated with it, came the miraculous Miller and Offenhauser engines, which were their legacy to racing. Some magnificent engineering, comparable only to Bugatti's work at Molsheim, came from Harry Armenius Miller, and there have been feats of driving and courage to equal anything seen in Europe.

For many years the cars, the Indianapolis 'roadsters', were as different from European racing cars as chalk from cheese; but now, once again, the design patterns are converging. Just as ordinary American cars are now much nearer the European concept, so it is on the track; but the razamataz of the American circuit remains its own special quality. Even if Brooklands had survived and done its level best to keep up with the times, it is certain that the differences between Brooklands and The Brickyard would be every bit as great as they appear to be on the following pages.

47 Nothing can possibly give a better idea of the Brooklands slogan 'The right crowd and no crowding' than this picture taken in the earliest days. The neat enclosures, the white rails, the wooden seats, are all reminiscent of the racecourse, which it indeed set out to copy. The broad sweep of the banking in the background gives a marvellous sense of space, with the clubhouse on the left as the centre of social life.

48

49

48 The scene in the paddock makes a welcome change from the scene we are used to these days. This was the 1909 Whitsun Handicap at Brooklands.

49 Small boys and motor racing go hand in hand, and if your father is actually a racer, heaven is only round the corner. The car is a Lanchester 40hp with Master Rapson at the front and Mr Rapson at the other end. Mr Rapson made tyres among other things.

50 'Four little maids from school are we', and exactly what they were doing on the start line on 24 September 1907 is something history does not explain. The car is a Napier, which displays its number in the then required fashion, which was much easier for all to see. One feels that at least present-day commentators might be glad if the practice was revived.

51 This is one of the most famous of all Brooklands
figures, seen not in Weybridge but at Indianapolis,
where he drove this Bugatti in the '500' of 1923. He is
Count Louis Zborowski of Chitty Bang Bang fame.
He was killed in 1924 while driving a Mercedes at
Monza, and legend has it that he was wearing the
same cuff links as his father, Eliot Zborowski, had
been wearing when he too died in a Mercedes, at the
la Turbie hill-climb, when the links are said to have
caught in the hand throttle.

52 Before the start of the thirteenth annual Indianapolis '500' on 30 May 1925. The pace car, which
leads the pack round the track for their flying start, is
a Rickenbacker 8, driven by Louis Chevrolet. Across
the front of the grid are, left to right, Harry Hartz,
Pete de Paolo, the winner, (for the first time at over
100mph), and Leon Duray. The surface at that time
was still brick as can be clearly seen from the picture.

53

53 The 1927 start with some fine vintage menswear as well as interesting cars. On the front row, left to right again, Leon Duray's Miller, (one of the cars that Griffith Borgeson found in the Bugatti works, took back to America and painstakingly restored to its 'as new' condition), Pete de Paolo again, also in a Miller, and Frank Lockhart who had qualified at over 120mph. Lockhart died in 1928 when attempting the World Land Speed Record at Daytona beach in the Stutz *Black Hawk* of his own design and building.

54 There can be no more startling contrast to the excitement of Indianapolis than the studied amateur calm of Brooklands in 1924. Here is 'Ebby', (A. V. Ebblewhite), complete in coat and hat, pipe in mouth and stopwatches in box ready to start a handicap race. In later years he used a small Union Jack instead of the plain flag seen here. He used to wander across the track and stand by the first car off, give a little quick wave of the flag and then, as it roared away, move on to the next car, or next group of cars. There is something weirdly exciting about a handicap race as visitors to present day Vintage events will know. The car in mid-field being cranked is one of the rare RLSS Alfa Romeos and further over a Hyper Sports Lea-Francis.

55 Here are a selection of drivers and cars from the vintage period of Indianapolis, fabulous men and fabulous machines, each one of them set on winning a fabulous purse. This is Benny Shoaf with a Duesenberg, sporting a special intercooler for its supercharger, the work of Dr Sanford Moss.

59

56   Lou More who later built the Blue Crown Special which became an Indianapolis victor, here seen with the Coleman Special, which was a three-litre, four-cylinder Miller. He crashed on the north-east turn on the twenty-third lap.

57   Another Miller under the skin, but this time more mutilated than usual. Pete Kreis in 1928 with the Marmon Special, a car which had previously run as a Cooper, (no connection with the present day company of that name).

59   This is a story of dashed hopes. Fred Merzey with this strange-looking Coleman four-wheel-drive car, failed to qualify in 1932. That would have been bad luck just once, but poor Merzey never got into the race — ever.

58   1926, and this time a rear-drive Miller driven by John Duff and called the Elgar Special — he finished ninth.

60 Joe Caccia in the Alberti Special, which was in fact a modified Model A Duesenberg road car. He crashed in the thirty-fourth lap on this occasion, and was later killed during pre-race practice.

61 Back to Brooklands and one of the famous relay races. There was nothing you could do at a prep-school that you could not do at Brooklands. Ebby on the right getting ready for the start, with furled Union Jack, a Riley, an MG, and between them a Vale Special, a very low-built sports car, which came from a mews in Maida Vale and used Triumph parts. It would not 'pull the skin off a rice pudding', but it *looked* simply super!

62 Here is the Vale Special in action. Not fast, perhaps, but more reliable than the Amilcar on the grass. The latter is one of the very fast six-cylinder twin-cam, supercharged cars that have now become very much collectors' pieces.

63 Pit signals during a race are always supposed to convey everything necessary to the driver as he flashes past, and nothing at all to the people in the surrounding pits. All too often in the course of history the exact opposite has been the effect, but here at least it is the boss himself, Louis Coatalen, who is waving no less than three flags and looking fairly fierce along with it. Perhaps something like, 'If you expect a pay cheque at the end of this race you'd better go a damned sight faster than you are now', or, judging by the anxiety on the faces of some of the onlookers, perhaps, 'Come home all is forgiven', is nearer the mark. These are the Talbot-Darracq pits at the British Grand Prix of 1927.

64 When it really comes to signals there is nothing to beat the radio. This would appear to be the first radio-controlled racing car, and here one can see the set, the batteries and the microphone; the headset is in the leather helmet on the radio itself. The car dates back to 1932 and was, as you might have guessed, at Indianapolis. It is the Samson Special and was entered by Alder Samson, who was in the radio business.

65 Another view of the Samson Special which was in reality a Miller, but a very unusual one. It is a V16 made by Miller out of two of his straight-eight, 2-litre blocks on a common crankcase; Riley Brett was the mechanic. The car was driven by the three-times Indianapolis winner, Lou Meyer, who later became the Meyer of Meyer-Drake, who took over the mantle of Miller engineering when Miller died. And that mantle was quite something. Those who believe that only Europe could have produced Bugatti should take one look at the beautiful spherical fuel tank and the general standards of workmanship on the car. In Europe they could, at that time, have done as well, but no better.

66 It is part of the charm of race circuits that so much goes on behind the scenes. Here is an earnest discussion on the subject of carburettor float chambers in 1931, not presumably for the Austin Seven on whose bonnet the consultation is taking place, since its pistons are only that size. Do not overlook the charming caracature on the left-hand door.

67 Miller in all his glory seen here, (on the right), talking to Jimmy Murphy, who won the first post-war French Grand Prix in a Duesenberg, among countless other victories. The car is a rear-wheel-drive, 122cu in Miller, with normal aspiration by four two-throat Miller carburettors. It is a classic Miller in the making.

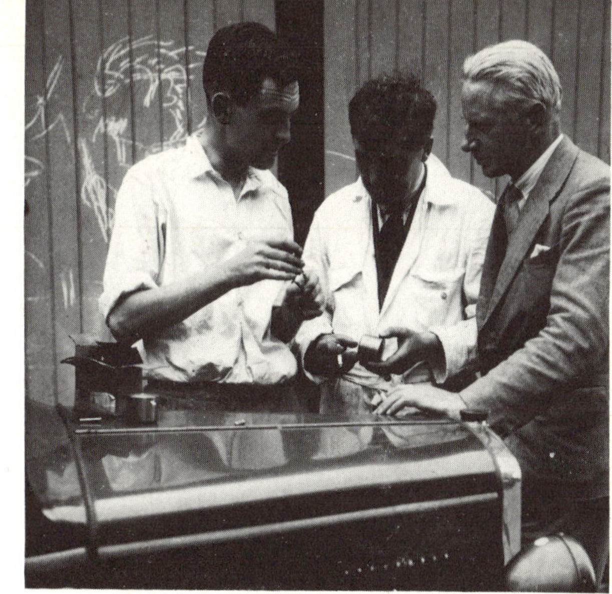

66

67

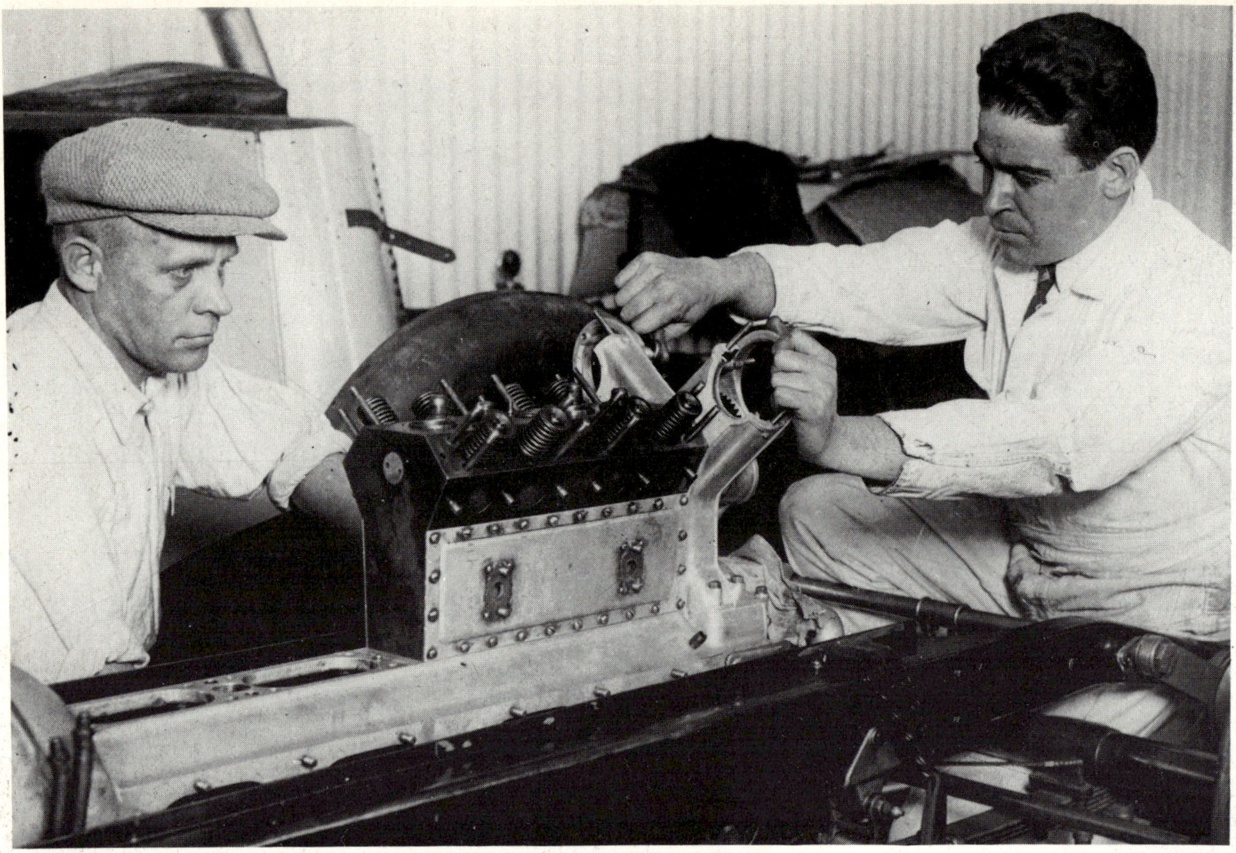

68

69

70

68 On the left is Ernie Olsen who was Murphy's riding mechanic at Le Mans with Bennet Hill, a driver of the late twenties. The car is again a rear-drive Miller.

69 This car was a product of Brooklands but not intended to race there. The 1938 Railton-Mobil Special was designed by Reid Railton, on the right, to capture the World Land Speed Record. It was driven by John Cobb, on the left, and did so comfortably. As the record attempts took place in America, and since soon after finishing this job in 1938 Reid Railton himself became a senior engineer with the Hudson company, it is very much an Anglo-American situation. The car had an 'S'-shaped frame with two engines, one driving the front wheels, the other the back. About six men were needed to lift the body off so that the driver could get in — or out!

70 The first rear-engined car to run at Indianapolis. It is 1937 and the car is a Vl6 Marmon here seen with Lee Oldfield at the wheel. It arrived late at the circuit and failed to qualify. Presumably, had it run, there would have been rather more coachwork to be fitted on, though it would hardly have disguised the some-what makeshift construction. The pipe from the radiator to the engine hardly looks like engineering of the Miller standard.

71

71 Another Indianapolis oddity and also rear-engined. The 1939 Gulf No-Nox Special ran on pump petrol when everyone else was using alcohol, which did not improve its chances. It was driven by George Bailey who was killed the following year. It was a rear-engined, four-wheel-drive Miller, but one feels that the old man was past his prime. He had been commissioned to make the cars by Gulf Oil, and he needed some money at the time; there was actually rarely a time when he did not. Four cars were built with the only six-cylinder engines Miller ever made and they ran at Indianapolis in 1939, 1940 and 1941 but none of them ever completed a race. An interesting but rather sad end to the Miller story. He died in 1943.

72 and 73 There can hardly be a greater contrast between these two scenes in the pits not long before a race. Brooklands with nothing in sight but a Baby Austin, and Indianapolis with, in the foreground, one of the unusual foreign visitors. The P3 Alfa Romeo in the foreground was driven by Louis Tomei and entered by Frank Griswald. It finished fifteenth in 1939. In the background is the famous Pagoda.

72

73

74 and **75**   Two more Indianapolis oddities. The six-wheeled Pat Clamcy Special which finished twelfth in 1948 and used one of the famous Offenhauser engines, as did the other car driven by Jimmy Daywalt in 1955. The latter had a Kurtis frame and was originally made with a 'Golden Arrow' fairing along each side. For some reason these were abandoned before the race and the car ran as shown.

76   Over the years there were many aspirants from Europe. After a fine beginning, with victory in their pockets, there was a period when it seemed impossible to get the right approach from the other side of the Atlantic. Here is Christian Werner in a works Mercedes in 1923.

77

77 Maconin Mario Umberto Borzacchini was born in Terni in 1899, and had a distinguished career as a racing driver mainly with Maserati and Alfa Romeo cars. He became a great friend of Nuvolari and died in a crash at Monza in 1933. Here he is at Indianapolis in 1930 with a sixteen-cylinder Maserati. In the centre, standing behind the car in a cap, is Ernesto Maserati, one of the famous brothers. The car had no luck and was obviously not going well. After four laps Rossi took over the wheel and it retired on the seventh lap with ignition trouble.

78 Luther Johnson and his mechanic Jimmy Lowden in their already outdated Bugatti which failed to qualify in 1936. In fairness to Bugatti it cannot be overlooked that the car was already out-classed, and anyway the great success of Bugatti was based as much on roadholding, braking and general handling as on anything else; qualities which were quite unnecessary on the Indianapolis circuit.

79 After the war, in 1946, Robert Arbuthnot took over one of the V12 Lagondas that W. O. Bentley had built to race at Le Mans just before the war, when they had put up a very creditable show. Anything less suited to Indianapolis it is hard to imagine, so that the car's failure to qualify comes as no surprise.

82

80 The famous Gasoline Alley at Indianapolis. The year is 1961, the car the Hoover Motor Express Special, a name which, as usual at this circuit, disguises something much more comprehensible in engineering terms. It is a Kurtis chassis with a tilted Offey engine, its power-train off-set to the right. Low down on the front of the chassis the socket for the electric motor used for starting can be seen. The three-eared hub nuts were originated by Ted Halibrand, also famous for the car's magnesium wheels.

81 Parnelli Jones in the pits in 1963. The car again a four-cylinder, Offey-engined special, this time known as the Agajanian Special.

82 The famous four-wheel-drive Novi entered by that most colourful of all Indianapolis entrants, Andy Granatelli. Note the special Indianapolis-type tyre treads for continuous left-hand turning. Leaning over the car in a dark pullover is British racing driver Tony Rolt, at that time much concerned with the Fergusson four-wheel-drive developments, and this was the system that Granatelli had built into the Novi when he took it over. The cars had originally been front-wheel-drive models. Unhappily it was dogged by oil trouble in the race.

83

83 A line-up of different approaches at Indianapolis. The year is 1963 and on the left is one of Mickey Thompson's cars with Mickey Thompson standing behind it. In the centre, Roger Ward sitting in the car with his mechanic A. J. Watson standing behind, and on the right, Colin Chapman standing beside his Lotus car with Dan Gurney at the wheel.

84

85

84 Quite a different line-up at Brooklands in 1937. This time it is the two new Murray Jamieson designed, twin-cam Austin Seven racers with, on this side of them, the side-valve model still raced in the team by the famous woman driver Kay Petre. The other drivers are Charles Goodacre and Bert Hadley.

85 Looking more like today, but still only the late thirties, the paddock at Brooklands with Kenneth Evans, in the white cap, pushing out his P3 Alfa Romeo, modified to have independent suspension. The Evans family, including sister Doreen, were very much part of the scene. They had a garage in South West London.

86 Another Brooklands speciality was the presence of bookmakers. It all presumably went back to the horse racing image, but they were always there, always welcome, and as usual always better informed than the punters. But it could go wrong as the picture in a later chapter shows.

87 On off-race days there was always something interesting going on at Brooklands. Here Cortese had brought over one of the new Alfa Romeo racing sports cars to be photographed by Klemantaski, who here posed beside him for someone else to work the shutter.

88 and **89**   When something goes wrong at sea you have to pump, when something went wrong at Brooklands someone else had to push (MG C-type), and if you could not make it go you called it plug trouble (Austin Seven racer).

3 BETWEEN THE WARS

When Mussolini paid the piper, but Hitler called the tune

So much happened between the two World Wars to highlight man's incredible aptitude for folly, that there can be little wonder in the news that Grand Prix racing was in the same kind of mess as the rest of human endeavour. It all started rather well, with Jimmy Murphy coming over from America with a Duesenburg to win the French Grand Prix. It went on with Bugatti reaping all the honours with a 'same-as-you-can-buy' Grand Prix car, which won all the unimportant races and rather fewer of those that mattered. In this period, too, comes Lory's famous eight-cylinder Delage, later to have a second life in a second formula, of which more later. And after all that the collapse of the whole Grand Prix system, and several years of anarchy; but not before Jano, at Alfa Romeo, had managed to get some splendid ideas off the drawing board and into reality.

The situation began to make sense again at the start of the thirties and Jano's thinking was at its apogee in 1932 with the creation of the 'Monoposto' Type B, usually known as the P3. By this time single-seaters had been accepted as the organisers had decided that as so many mechanics had been killed the drivers must race alone. The halcyon year was 1932, in which Nuvolari, and often Caracciola, were unbeatable. There was a set-back in the following year when Alfa Romeo was virtually nationalised and the racing team was withdrawn, the effort was taken over by Ferrari with his Scuderia Ferrari, the prancing horse replacing the four-leaf clover. All this publicity for Italy, and all the triumph that 'Il Duce' made of them, irritated Hitler, who had by then seized power in Germany, and he offered large sums of money for success in that field.

By 1934 a new formula was due, and it was one which admirably suited the Führer and one sometimes wonders how much influence he had had on it. It was a formula not of engine size but of weight. Within certain prescribed limits of size, anything could be built as long as it did not weigh more than 750 kilogrammes. This of course is a formula where money is almost as important as brains, for simplicity and low weight cost money, and Hitler had more money than Mussolini, or at least larger presses for printing it.

Two German teams, Mercedes and Auto Union, entered the fray, and much has been written about them for those who are interested in the full story. Both had their share of top drivers, both had personalities of great interest, Dr Ferdinand Porsche and Alfred Neubauer among them. Alfa Romeo managed to retain their leading position during the first year of the new rules (1934), but from then until the war broke out it was a German benefit.

The British unfortunately never really got a look in; with insufficient money to buy the string and canvas to make one more squadron for the RAF, and without even the willingness to pay for a victory in the Schneider Trophy it was pointless looking for Government backing. The rich had Brooklands, where the dry martinis were at least as good as the racing, so why worry? Fortunately one or two people did, with interesting results. There was by then what we should now call a Formula Two, only it was called a Voiturette Formula; and the cars were limited to 1,500cc. Here it was thought something might be done, and Raymond Mays, with Humphrey Cooke's finance and Peter Berthon's design, produced the English Racing Automobile (ERA), and swept the voiturette field. Mays himself also made light work of the hill climb scene.

Into the middle of all this came Richard Seaman, who set out on his own to beat the ERAs at their own game. He bought an eight-cylinder Delage, which was then over eight years old, and got Gulio Ramponi to rebuild it for him. He then enjoyed a glorious season with it before being invited to drive for Mercedes Benz. The tragedy of his death at Spa is perhaps mitigated by the thought that had he lived his loyalties would have been sorely stretched on the outbreak of war, for he was an undoubted Englishman, but he had married a German girl and was wholly loyal to his Mercedes team. There are times when politics seem even worse than sponsorship.

90   As soon as World War I was over motor racing
started again, and once more Fiat made a good deal of
the running. Many of the men were the famed drivers
of the pre-war years, but there were new men besides,
and here is Fiat's line-up for 1921. In the back row
(standing) are, left to right, Bruno, Romassoto Lam-
piano, Nazzaro (who had shaved off his moustache),
Bordino, Giaccone, and Masino, while on the ground
in front are an unnamed man on the left and Carig-
nano beside him.

91   A little wheel changing during one of the tests of
the prototype Fiat 804 during 1922. In the foreground are Nazarro on the right, with his mechanic,
Bordino, on the left. Cavalli, from the design staff, in
hat and coat behind.

92 At the Italian Grand Prix in 1922 Salamano with his mechanic, Bruno, in the Fiat 803. The race was won by Bordino with Nazarro second, both in similar cars.

93 Giaccone at the 1922 Targa Florio where he was fifth in a Fiat 501 SS. Seen here talking to Giovanni Agnelli, the founder and director of Fiat.

94 and **95** As may be imagined the Germans did not find it easy to get back into racing in the early years after World War I, but some of the pre-war Benz cars appeared in various parts of Europe, including Brooklands. In 1923, however, the Benz company made a serious bid for Grand Prix honours, and produced a very futuristic car, designed by Edmund Rumpler. This had the engine at the back, (and thereby foreshadowed Auto Union), with the radiator mounted in a curve above it, complete with streamlined header tank. It had a two-litre, six-cylinder engine and four-wheel brakes. It made but one appearance in a Grand Prix at Monza, and, of the team of three, two managed to be fourth and fifth. Later one of the cars ran with road equipment as a sports model, for which, as the pictures show, not much modification was necessary.

96 While the Germans were pressing ahead Fiat were content to stay in the mainstream, even to be a little old fashioned as this 501 SS from 1923 shows. A slightly modified touring car, it still has the bolster fuel tank and the two sloping spare wheels which graced the cars of a decade, and a world war, before.

96

97 Alfa Romeo on the other hand were producing some very elegant racing machinery, and were indeed going to go on doing so for the whole of the inter-war period. This car, from 1923, is the RL Targa Florio model, now in the new and splendid Alfa Romeo Museum. The car was specially made for the event and the company's efforts were rewarded by first, second and fourth places as well as the fastest lap. The car was designed by Merosi.

97

98 A final fling from Fiat, the monster to end all monsters, and usually known as *Mefistofele*. It started life as a record car, which Nazzaro used at Brooklands in 1908, after which it had a rather mysterious lapse from public sight. It reappeared briefly in 1921 in the hands of a certain John Buff and was then acquired by Ernest Eldridge, who took the original engine out, and replaced it with a six-cylinder aero engine of 21,714cc! This meant adding a bit to the chassis as well and it is said, but not confirmed, that two sections from the side of a London bus frame were used. Eldridge broke the World Land Speed Record with it in July 1924 at 146·01mph, after which the car went into honourable retirement and is now in the Fiat Centro Storico in Turin. The present tyres are modern: the, 'reinforced for heavy service . . .', makes charming reading. Note, too, the levers drilled for lightness and the handle fitted above the shock absorbers to enable the driver to get out.

98

D.M.G. 3917

99 The difficult-to-handle, 2 litre, eight-cylinder Mercedes seen here with Otto Mertz at the wheel. Mertz was for many years a Mercedes works driver, though not one of the better known ones. He had been chauffeur to Archduke Ferdinand of Austria, (whose murder at Sarajevo had given the signal for the start of World War I), and was in fact driving the Archduke's own car, second in the procession, when it happened. It was he who carried his dying master into a nearby house for protection. He later returned to Mercedes and did well in hill-climbs, making the fastest time of the day at both Solitude and Klausen in 1924.

100 Here is the same car making its debut at Monza in 1924. Mercedes entered four cars driven by Werner, Count Masetti, Neubauer and Zborowski. The last named was killed in a crash during the race, and Mercedes withdrew the team — they were not doing very well anyhow. This is Werner in the pits. Like Mertz in the previous picture, he was a works driver in the Mercedes experimental and racing de-partment, and his drives were therefore somewhat restricted; but his victories in the Targa Florio and the Coppa Florio of the same year marked him out as a driver of real distinction. He later partnered Caracciola in both the Mille Miglia and the Le Mans 24-hour race. He died in 1932. There seems to be enough spilled fuel to start a very serious fire.

101 The famous racing driver has always had a special place in the public mind, not infrequently on the front page of the newspapers. The Sunday supplements in Italy on 12 July 1925 were no different, and here is the famous father of a famous son, Antonio Ascari, getting the treatment after winning the European Grand Prix at Spa.

La vittoria italiana nel Gran premio automobilistico d'Europa disputato a Spa. La macchina « Alfa Romeo » guidata da Antonio Ascari, che ha vinto la corsa alla velocità media di 120 chilometri all'ora, al suo arrivo al traguardo viene coperta del tricolore   (Disegno di Alfredo Ortelli).

102 Without designers no one would win a motor race at all, and without Vittorio Jano the whole face of motor racing would have been quite different. He is here seen standing in front of what is generally supposed to be his first masterpiece, the P2 Alfa Romeo, which he designed in 1924. At the other end of his career he designed the Grand Prix Lancias that were to become Ferraris. A giant figure in a world of giants.

103 A little group taken in the pits in 1922 which includes Nicola Romeo, the Romeo in Alfa Romeo, standing with a stick; leaning on the pit counter with a cap on is Merosi, while sitting smiling on the counter itself is none other than the youthful Enzo Ferrari.

104   Several years later, in 1932, on the occasion of the victorious debut of the 2·3 litre Monza model, also designed by Jano, there is this group. From left to right they are : Luigi Fusi, then on the Alfa engineering staff and now famous as the author of the great text-book on Alfas ; Colombo, another of the big Alfa design men ; Enzo Ferrari ; Jano, with his arm round his son, and his wife on his left ; Mrs Prato and Prato, who was Alfa's works manager.

105   Felice Nazzaro in overalls, and without the moustache of his earlier years, talks to W. F. Bradley, a very significant figure in motor racing in the years between the wars, and indeed for long after. He was *Autocar*'s European correspondent and a friend of Bugatti. Besides being a journalist of note he was more than something of an entrepreneur, and was mixed up in all kinds of team affairs as manager or adviser. He died in the South of France not so many years ago, at an age of well over 90, and, since his death, the motoring world is beginning to divide itself into those who still feel his word is law, and a later school, who have some doubts about the veracity of many of his statements, hitherto regarded as historical fact.

106 and 107   Two track versions of the SSK Mercedes. After the comparatively lightweight, and one might almost say Italianate, two-litre Mercedes the SSKs were monsters. Mercedes had just joined with Benz by that time. The second picture shows Otto Mertz at the wheel again in a more refined version really intended for tracks such as the Avus. It needed massive strength to drive these cars and Merz was often teamed with Caracciola. It was said that Merz could drive a six-inch nail into a board with his bare fist — for which exercise the Mercedes was probably good practice.

108   Fiat's racing swansong. They had more or less retired from racing in 1924, but made a brief comeback with this car in 1926-7. It had a twelve-cylinder engine made of two blocks of six, with the crankshafts geared together, and several other unusual features. Note the flat top of the steering wheel so that the driver could see where he was going, and the wire gauze to protect him from flying oil, but still allow him to see the instruments. It only ran once, in the 1927 Milan Grand Prix, which it won. From this point on Italian racing was in the hands of Alfa Romeo, which in 1933 became state owned as part of the IRI (Institute for Industrial Reconstruction), and about that time too, Benito Mussolini started to use motor racing as national publicity.

109   The first of the Jano-designed, eight-cylinder racing cars was the Monza with strong sports car affiliations; it even ran every now and then with wings and lamps. It was the beginning of Italian domination in a field which, for a brief moment at least, looked as if it belonged to Bugatti. But 1931 was not Bugatti's year and when it came to the Monza Grand Prix Alfa Romeo fielded four cars. Two twelve-cylinder cars (twin sixes — the Italians seemed to like that idea), and two of the new 2·3-litre Monzas. Nuvolari, seen here, was originally at the wheel of one of the twelve-cylinder cars, but that broke down. The other had crashed in practice killing its driver Arcangeli; Alfa Romeo would have withdrawn from the race but they had a cable form 'Il Duce' which simply told them to start and win, so

they did. When Nuvolari's car broke down he joined Campari, and is here seen filling the car before handing over to his co-driver. Close scrutiny of the front of the car would show that it had not yet been given its famous Monza grille, combining a new radiator shape with the stoneguard.

110   For the enthusiast a more usual view of the Monza Alfa Romeo with the correct front end. At the wheel is 'Phi-phi' Etancelin, on the occasion of the Picardy Grand Prix of 1933, which he won.

109

110

111

112

111 Nuvolari, perhaps the greatest driver of all. Coming after Nazarro, and before Fangio, who can say if he was better than either? Who can say if James Clark or Mario Andretti have the edge on him or not? Tiny, volatile, and quite indomitable, he raced as hard on inadequate cars at the back of the field as he did when equipped with a more or less certain winner. Wild in antics in the cockpit, curious in dress, brave as a lion, he was an idol for the whole of Italy and most of Europe. Having, for example, crashed a P2 Alfa Romeo when giving it a try-out, he was, literally,

hoisted, a few days later, on to his Bianchi motor-cycle, in plaster and bandages, to win the Grand Prix des Nations. He is said to have invented the four-wheel drift and is reputed to have done so well with the P3 Alfa Romeo's (which had very poor brakes) because he said brakes were no good and only made you go slower, and he never used them. He won the 1935 German Grand Prix against all odds, and a British TT in an MG Magnette when, a day before, he had not seen the car or even tried a pre-selector gearbox. He always wore round his neck a little gold tortoise given him by the Italian soldier/poet, Gabriele d'Annunzio, as a symbol of prudence and steady progress. After the war he suffered with a complaint that made petrol fumes a danger to him, but he drove his last race at Monte Pellegrino when he was already fifty-eight and died at his home in Mantua in 1953, when he was sixty-one.

112, 113 and **114**   Some shots of the famous P3 Alfa Romeo which for a year or so swept the field in Europe, and made the running for Mussolini. The shadow of future events appears in these pictures, as the driver is none other than Caracciola, soon to become a leader of the German opposition. He is seen before the start at Tripoli in 1932, on the starting line at Monza, and in the pits during the Monza race, also in 1932. The man on the left in the last picture, wearing what were in those days called 'co-respondent' shoes, appears not to like the camera prying too closely lest it should give the lie to the idea that it was only plug trouble.

115

115   Once Hitler had decided to beat Mussolini at his own game, Alfa Romeo had to try to match the German cars. But as Il Duce had rather less ready money than the Führer, they were in some difficulty. Here is one of the later Alfa Romeos with roughly the same engine bored-out to a greater capacity, and with coachwork which may not have helped it to go any faster, but looked more in keeping with the style Mercedes Benz had created. This is Nuvolari after winning at Budapest in 1935, the same year that, in the same car, he beat the Germans in their own Grand Prix by nothing more or less than sheer driving. He won nearly fifty major motor races between 1924 and 1946, including the Mille Miglia, Le Mans, the TT, and countless Grands Prix, mostly with Alfa Romeo.

116   Nuvolari on the left talking to Caracciola, who, despite his Italian sounding name, was a German driver. Rudolf Caracciola was born in 1901 and started racing in 1922. When the Mercedes company withdrew from racing in 1931 he joined Alfa Romeo, and stayed with them until he re-joined Mercedes in 1934. This picture dates from the Alfa Romeo period.

117 and 118 Another of the great German drivers was Bernd Rosemeyer, this time with Auto Union. Seen here with one of the Auto Union engineers, and in front of his specially built 5-litre, straight-eight Horch Coupé. His fame rests entirely on his driving for the Auto Union team. He was born in Lingen in 1909 and only raced cars for three years. He had been in the DKW motorcycle team (DKW was also part of Auto Union), and bullied and badgered his way into the car team. He first drove in 1935 and quickly became the acknowledged master of these rear-engined cars which were so difficult to handle. Only Nuvolari in later years was anything like as expert. He was killed tragically in January 1938 when trying to beat the newly-made Mercedes Class B Flying Kilometer record. His car was blown off course and hit one of the concrete bridges over the Autobahn on which the record attempt was being made.

119 Throughout the later part of the decade Auto Union usually had to play second fiddle to Mercedes, but from the beginning they chose some first-class drivers. In the earliest days they 'went Italian' and bought the services of Achille Varzi, whose love/hate relationship with Nuvolari was a legend. Here he is, as immaculate as ever, at the wheel of one of the early cars. It was much more consciously rear-engined than a modern Grand Prix car and it was very difficult to feel what the back end was doing until sometime after it had done it, which was usually too late.

120 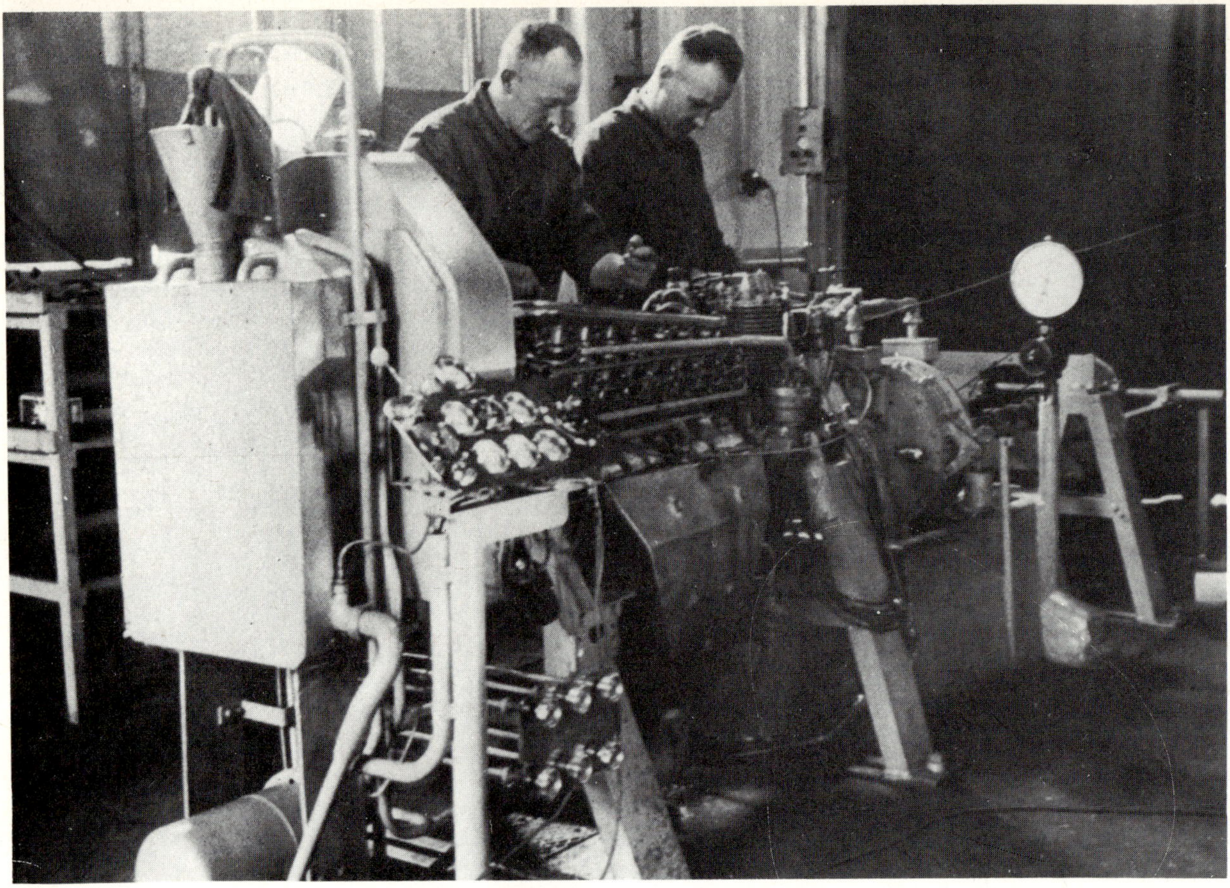

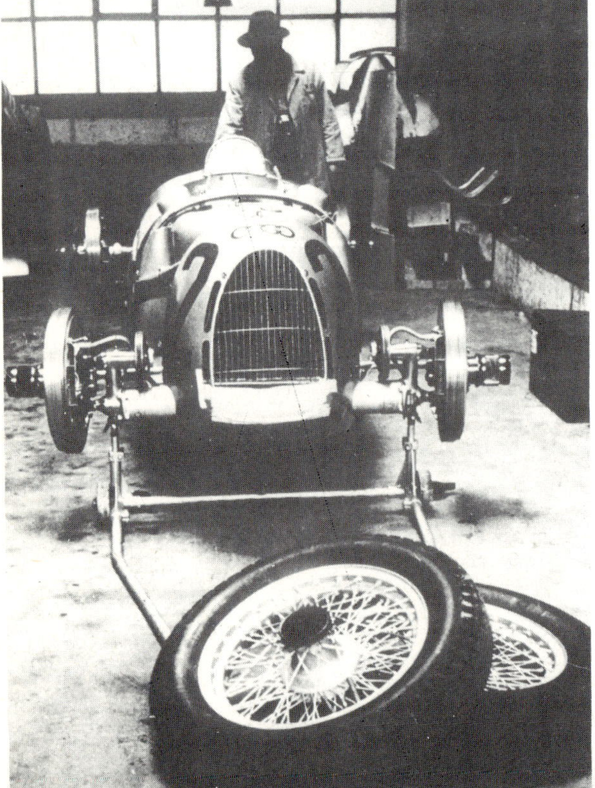

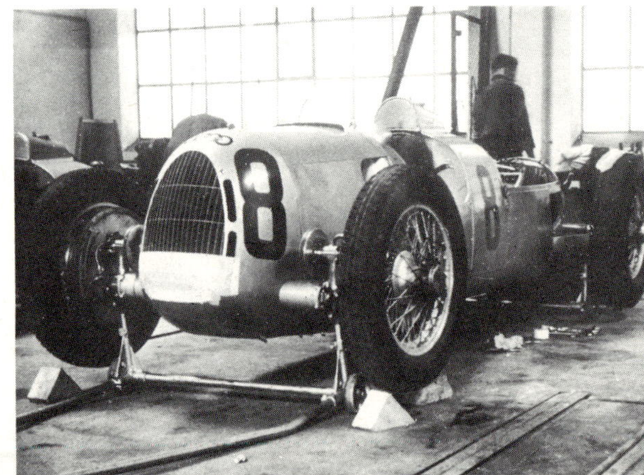

121

120 To make a change from the men, here are the Auto Unions on their way from the factory to the circuit. An engine on the test bed

121 The car begins to take shape

122 Wheels, and most of the works, are now in place.

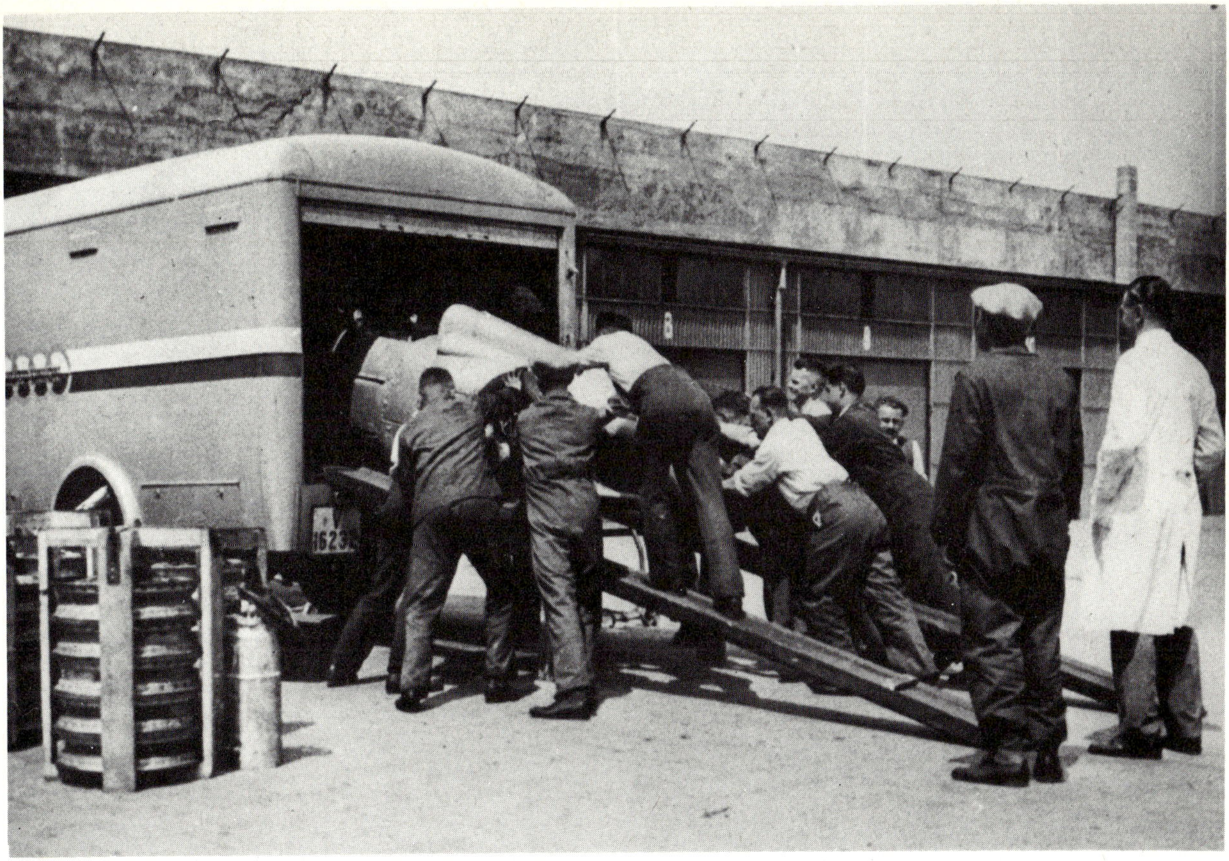

123

123 Manhandling a car onto a transporter, although it might have been easier to use a winch!

124 Arrival at the circuit. With three cars for the race and two to act as stand-bys and for practice this does give some idea of the scale of operations and the amount of money involved. There was no sponsor, of course, unless you count the Nazi Party, but against this amount of money, (never mind the skill), there was not much Alfa Romeo, Bugatti or Maserati could possibly do about it.

125

125   The scene did not change much over the years, but these are the later Auto Unions with more in front of the driver and less behind, so that although the handling was little different it felt better. These are mechanics warming up before a German Grand Prix.

126   A plan view of the car with mechanics at work. The steering-wheel had to come out to get the driver in, so it was readily detachable.

127   By contrast, but how similar, the Mercedes pits with cars being prepared. These are the earliest, 1934, models which were much higher built than the later more powerful cars, but all same, victors from the word go.

128 Mercedes victories were largely the work of one man, seen here standing beside Lang's car at the 1938 German Grand Prix. He is Alfred Neubauer, Mercedes team manager, both before and after the war and himself at one time a racing driver. Born in 1891, he was Mercedes team manager from 1926 to 1955, having joined Austro-Daimler as a test driver after serving in the German forces in World War I. He gave up racing and took to management in the year Mercedes joined Benz, and never has a company had a more faithful and successful servant, or drivers a more authoratative and understanding manager.

129 Here he is (extreme left) a few months later at the Italian Grand Prix at Monza, walking out on to the starting line with Caracciola's car, one of the lower and later 1938 models.

130, 131 and **132**   As with the Fiat in an earlier chapter, a look at the car helps one to understand the men who made it and the men who fought with it. In all its splendid detail, this is the later 1938 Auto Union with a three-litre, three-camshaft, twelve-cylinder engine (designed by Feuereissen and von Eberhorst, who after the war worked for Jowett) and not the original Porsche-designed V16.

133 Auto Union started the season with the new engine in the old car and facing the death of Rosemeyer; but later when a new body had been evolved, and Nuvolari had joined the team, they got their spirits back and started winning again, which was natural enough for Nuvolari, seen here enjoying the fruits of it.

134 Racing drivers are not unlike fighter pilots, except that there are perhaps fewer of them, and the stories they tell are often in the same vein. Wartime airmen were laughed at for their stories that began, 'there I was at ten thousand feet, with nothing on the clock but the maker's name'. This is Caracciola in the pits before the German Grand Prix of 1937 at Nurburgring, telling what must have been the father of that tale.

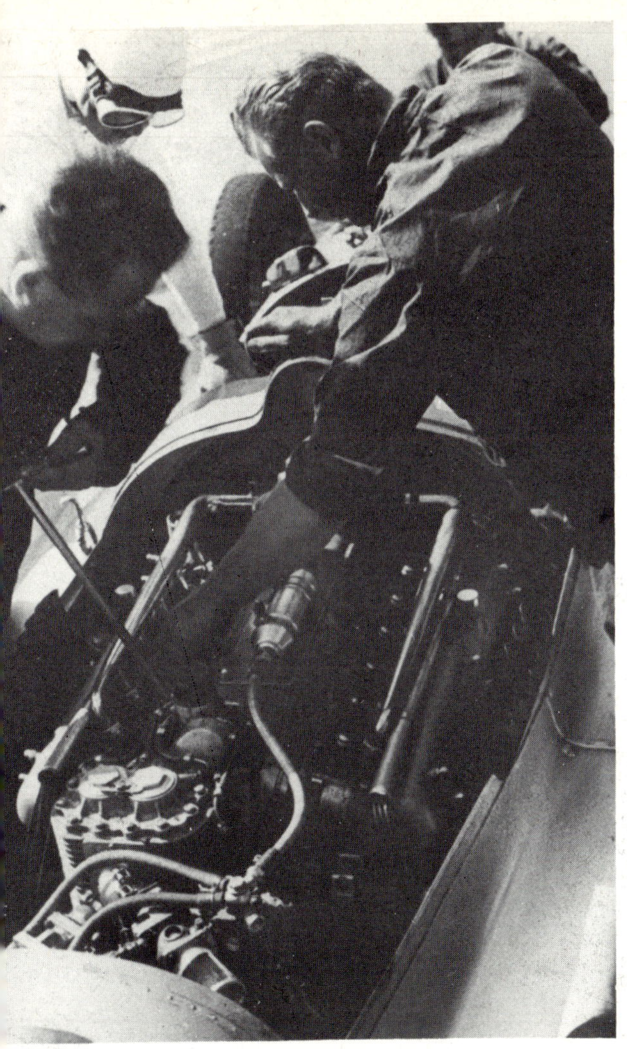

135   The testing and setting up of a car has not changed that much over the years, but one must suppose that it is a business of ever-increasing complication. Here Hans von Stuck's mechanics are at work on his Auto Union prior to a race.

136   With sixteen cylinders needing sixteen plugs there was more than enough screwing up and unscrewing as 'warming-up' plugs were changed for 'hotter' racing ones. All the driver can do is watch and wait and try not to bite his finger-nails.

137 Even when the car is ready the officials often are not, or practise is suspended for the moment and all the driver can do is wait. This is Hans von Stuck doing just that. In the background is Witney Straight's transporter. Straight was at that time using a modified monoposto Maserati painted in blue and white, the American racing colours. He had little hope of winning but as a wealthy amateur he lent much colour to the racing scene.

138 In the background, listening and watching the clocks, is Dr Porsche, the Auto Union designer, creator of the Volkswagen, and later the cars which still bear his name. One of the greatest designers, he was not without his follies, and many might be tempted to say the Auto Union was one of them; for it was not until he had gone and Feuereissen and Eberan von Eberhorst redesigned the car that it really came on to form.

139 This shot of Caracciola after winning the Tripoli Grand Prix in 1935 is a constant reminder that Mercedes were top dogs, and as much *über alles* as Germany itself.

140 In this pre-war heyday of motor racing, pit stops were an integral part of every race, and not as they are today a sure sign that all is not well and that the chances of victory are now negligible. Everyone in those days made at least one pit stop, as fuel was always needed and, more often than not, tyres. Crews became so expert at the job that if a car came in for anything at all it was worth changing the tyres, since it usually cost no more time. The speed of pit work was indeed often enough a step in the direction of the winner's flag. The following pictures show pit stops by both teams and give a fair idea of the fever pitch of excitement that went with them. A seat in the grandstand, opposite the pits, was worth every penny you paid for it. The car approaches and is given a clear indication of where to stop. Overshooting the pits is a disastrous waste of valuable seconds.

141 After a much needed drink and some news from the Auto Union team manager fuel is replenished and the two mechanics at the rear change the old wheels (the front wheels will not be changed), while the driver wipes his goggles. With a last bang at the off-side rear wheel, another quick gulp and a check that the bonnet is fixed, the flag marshall will wave the car back on to the circuit.

142 The same thing at Mercedes-Benz, taken incidentally at Donington in 1937, during one of the two British Grands Prix to which the Germans came. This first picture is actually pre-race and shows the old way of filling the tank with churns. This resulted in so much spillage that in the actual race some kind of pressure pipe was always used.

143 The race itself with the new rear wheels on and the fuel almost in; Neubauer, watch in hand, surveys the scene.

144

145

144 A push start back into the race and one can clearly see how much fuel is spilled on the car despite the pipe.

145 The German visits to Donington were the highlights of the British season and everyone was there. On the left, the tall figure is Richard Seaman standing next to Witney Straight, who is smoking a cigarette, and, arms folded, in overalls in the foreground, is Charlie Martin, a well-known Brooklands Bugattiste.

146 As was the British custom, bookies were in the paddock. Unfortunately the result was something of a foregone conclusion, since either Mercedes or Auto Union were bound to win, and everyone had a pretty good idea which driver in each team it would be. The bookies therefore found it expedient to leave shortly before the payout, and there were some ugly scenes. Facing the camera, and showing suitably British signs of distress when contronted with unsuitable social behaviour, is well-known journalist, record breaker, and sometime Public Relations Officer to the Austin Motor Co, Alan Hess.

147 As the European dictators had made motor racing an essential part of the propaganda instrument, it was necessary to explore all the possibilities that existed on the periphery of racing itself, and among these was obviously record breaking. Records seem to have gone out of fashion these days, but in the thirties they were very much the thing. Mercedes-Benz therefore modified one of their later twelve-cylinder Grand Prix cars and fitted it with a special body as seen here. Caracciola set up new Class D records with it on 9 February 1939, on the autobahn at Dessau. This came after the previous round of Class B records, (with the bigger-engined cars), that had resulted in Rosemeyer's tragic death in January 1938.

148 Here is Rosemeyer with that other famous holder and breaker, Major Goldie Gardner. This and the two subsequent pictures are not dated but they must have been taken a short while before the accident happened.

149 and 150 A long shot and a close up of Dr Porsche giving last minute instructions to his driver.

149

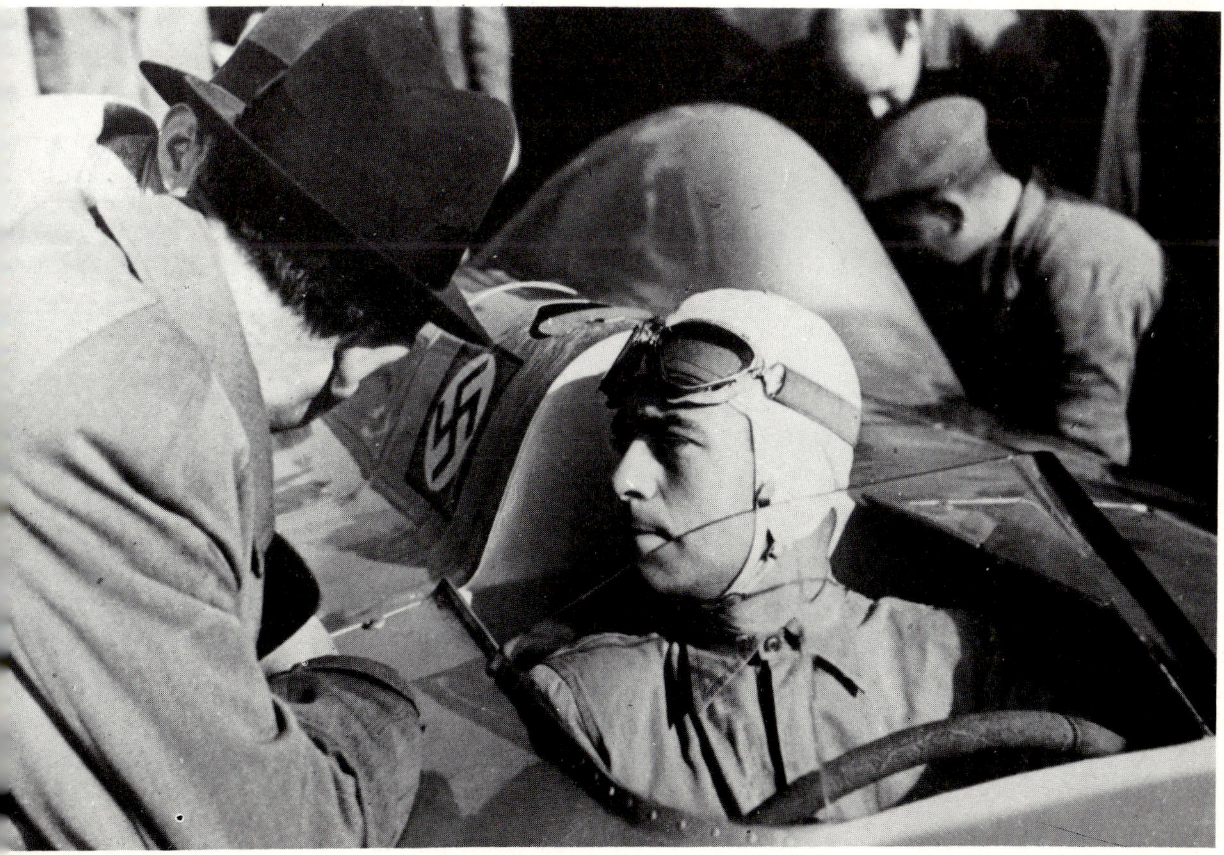

150

151

152

151   While the dictators poured money into the Grand Prix there was no room for amateurs or even professionals who lacked that essential commodity. But there were other fields, and spurred on by the generated enthusiasm of the big boys, there seemed to Humphrey Cooke and Raymond Mays to be a chance for England in the 1,500cc or Voiturette races, which so often preceded the main events. In this field Italy, in the shape of Maserati, had been reaping the honours, since Hitler had ousted them from the bigger scene. The ERA was, and still is, a unique concept. It was based on the 1,500cc Riley engine in a chassis designed by Reid Railton. Berthon modified the engine and Murray Jamieson looked after the supercharging. Once in its stride it was a huge success, and, although in all only seventeen cars were made, they took British prestige all over the world. It is an interesting quirk of statistics that in 1937 ERA gained more race victories than anyone, with fourteen to Mercedes-Benz's seven. All the same, the financial strain was enormous, and by 1939 Humphrey Cook could no longer afford to keep going and the works, as such, closed down, though the independents went on. Here are some of them. Peter Walker is seated in the car and Peter Whitehead is in the white shirt. They formed an impressive team. Prince Birabongse of Siam, a noted driver and known as 'Bira' is talking to Walker. Sitting in his own ERA on the right is Pat Fairfield, the South African, whose memorial can still be seen on the road to the paddock at Silverstone.

152   The only person and the only car to give the ERAs any real competition was Dick Seaman and his Delage. He had been a friend of Witney Straight at Cambridge and when Straight gave up professional racing Seamen went on, having acquired, through Straight, the services of Gulio Ramponi as a head mechanic, (he was a good deal more than that in present day parlance). On Ramponi's advice Seaman bought a 1927 Delage from Earl Howe, and Ramponi rebuilt and modified it. In the following season Seaman took four first places and set himself on the road which led to his being invited to join the Mercedes-Benz team. Here is Ramponi in the car on the way to the start line from the paddock. The top of his transporter can be seen in the background.

153   Almost as important to Raymond Mays as the Voiturette victories were his own performances in hill climbs, at which he was a past master. Here he is in the ERA in the paddock at Prestcott sheltering under the much needed umbrella which at least proclaims the name of his car and not a commercial sponsor.

154 Hill climbs were important in those days and important people attended them. Here, outside the time-keepers' hut at Prestcott, are Jean Bugatti on the left talking to Lord Howe, in the cap, and Jean-Pierre Wimille, the Bugatti driver.

155 With limited funds a great deal of interesting work went on, not the least of which were the two twin-cam Jamieson-designed Austins that we have already seen at Brooklands. Here is one of them being assembled in 1936. Whatever the British may have lacked it was neither enthusiasm nor skill, and to many the little Austins are a real highlight in racing car design.

156 On a much smaller scale many enthusiasts built Hill Climb Specials usually using motorcycle engines. Here is David Fry, who with his brother ran the *Frei-Keiserwagen*, named after its owner-drivers and Dick Caesar who designed it. The German part was a joke on Auto Union whose cars were often called Porsche-Wagens. There were others, too, like *Dorcas*, so named because in biblical terms she was full of good works, and countless others, perhaps the best known of which was John Bolster's *Bloody Mary* which is now in the National Motor Museum.

155

156

4 THE SPORTS CARS

Same as you can buy anywhere between Le Mans and Sebring

To try to find the exact point where sports cars and racing cars parted company is something of a problem. The first car to be called a 'sports' car by its makers, was the Prince Henry Vauxhall, which had after all competed in a very sporting event, the Prince Henry Trial. The first 'racing' car is generally held to be one of the early 'Canstat' Daimlers, since it had been built 'with racing in mind'; but certainly up to World War I there was a good deal of interchangeability.

After World War I Le Mans seemed to have been both the unifying and separating factor. The post war French Grand Prix, which in effect saw the revival of Grand Prix racing in Europe, was run there in 1921, and two years later in 1923 the famous 24-hour race for sports cars came into being. At least here we have an organisers' definition of what he saw as the difference. The race, which was the invention of Charles Faroux and Georges Durand, was intended to be for practical touring cars, (this might be difficult to believe nearly sixty years later, but it is true). In the beginning the regulations called for at least thirty cars exactly similar to the one entered to be in existence. If the car was of more than 1,100cc there had to be four seats, and ballast to the equivalent weight of the passengers had to be carried, together with all the tools and spares that were to be used in the race. For the first hour or two of the event the hood had to be erected, and at the very beginning only one man was permitted to work on the car — the driver! Le Mans changed over the years; but until quite recently the spirit remained the same, and even up to the Ford victory as late as 1969 there was some kind of relationship between the cars at Le Mans and sports cars that were on the general market. Certainly the Ferrari and Jaguar wins in the immediately preceding era were essentially with cars bearing a noticeable resemblance to their showroom products.

In the years between there were any number of sports car events, and any number of sports car races held among racing car events. Most of these had some relationship with Le Mans, but also a life in their own right, such as the TT and the Irish races. Out of them came the small sports cars for which first France and then Great Britain became famous. The number of small French sports cars at the end of the twenties was prodigious, even though they nearly all used the same proprietary engines. In Britain, starting with the MG, there were almost as many, and the Le Mans 'kit', consisting of two spare wheels behind a 'slab' tank with aero screens and stoneguards on the lamps, was *de rigeur*. The fact that most of them had little power, even in favourable circumstances, was neither here nor there. It is an interesting sidelight on the influence of fashion over design, that when William Lyons first introduced his SS Jaguar it was in copy of the prevailing French theme as epitomised by Delage; but when it came to his last *tour de force* before the war, in the form of the SS 100, it was the Le Mans idiom that prevailed.

There were, of course, many more amateurs in the realm of sports car racing, so that the paddock (and indeed the pit) often had a greater air of informality, as girl friends and uncles were as apt to form the crew as anyone else. Even though sponsors had not a toe-hold, there was an air of seriousness about the Grand Prix that was not so much in evidence even at Le Mans, where the lady in a bed of snakes, or Sunday morning Mass, was as much part of the scene as the many hospitality tents.

The Americans seem only to have discovered the sports car when they came to Europe during World War II, though one must not overlook such early joys as the Mercer 'Raceabout' and the 'Black Hawk' Stutz, but the 'sport car', as they chose to call it and certainly the small sports car was as new to them as was the idea that motoring could be fun.

When they went home after the war they took with them their MGs and a variety of other sports cars, and the whole movement proliferated into small and then big races, and into the return to Le Mans to try to beat the Europeans at their own game. Briggs Cunningham did not quite manage to, but after years of trying, through thick and thin, Ford did.

Now the sports car is disappearing from the roads and from the circuits. Sporting machinery is called GT for Grand Touring, though few of the cars could be grand to tour in. The races have been given over to prototypes which, admirable and exciting as they may be from a racing point of view, are as far removed from the sports car as a Grand Prix model of the thirties was from the district nurse's runabout. For this reason the old sports cars have become interesting, as their time is already past and only the photographs remain. What a picture they conjure up; one where pleasure was paramount and the sport was more important than winning.

157 Not perhaps the first sports car, not even the first sporting event, but these two intrepid French journalists drove their Lancia from St Petersburg (now Leningrad), to Paris, which must have proved something in terms of reliability, but little, it would appear, in terms of comfort.

158 We have noted in the introduction to this chapter that Vauxhall were the first to advertise one of their products as a sports car, and here they are living up to their reputation just before their last competition appearance in the 1922 TT. These were specially designed and prepared 3-litre models.

159

159   Just to show that the true racing car was only just around the corner here is one in 1922, with E. Swain at the wheel, without its mud-wings. It was from this model that Raymond Mays and Amherst Villiers developed the Vauxhall Villiers car with which Mays had so much success in hill-climbs.

160   A picture taken by Vincenzo Lancia himself of the first Lambda on road test in the mountains round Turin. The Bugatti-like radiator was dropped from the production models, but the *monocoq* construction which was years ahead of its time can clearly be seen.

161   Sports car racing in the grand manner came in the twenties, and here are two of the major figures in an Alfa Romeo 1,750 Super Sport. Campari is at the wheel and Gulio Ramponi in the passenger's seat. Ramponi later came to live in England and rebuilt the Delage for Richard Seaman in the mid-thirties. This is the car that won the 1929 Mille Miglia.

162   Another famous Mille Miglia occasion and Nuvolari at the controls of an Alfa Romeo 1,750 in 1930. His passenger is Guidotti who later became Alfa Romeo's racing manager.

161

Goodrich

Goodrich

TEX

162

163 This is one of those marvellous publicity pictures that can hardly have fooled any of the people any of the time. Said to be the three victorious Alfa Romeos at the finish of the Spa 24-hour Race in 1930, nothing about it seems to be authentic, not even the back flag for finishing! The cars and drivers are genuine, however, the cars themselves being 1,750s, and the three cars in winning order were driven by Marioni and Gherzi, Cortese and Ivanowski, Zehender and Canovesi.

164 The 1,750 Alfa Romeo and the Mille Miglia again, this time 1932, but the picture is here because it gives a marvellous evocation of the period. Back-to-front caps for Alferi and Cella in number fifty-five, and linen helmets for Givlay and Venturi in the car behind, and spectators all over the road.

165 Borzacchini was another famous name, seen here at the end of the 1932 Mille Miglia. He is at the wheel with Bignami, outright winners in an eight-cylinder 2·3-litre Alfa Romeo. At that time this was the epitome of Latin sports car design, the apple of every young man's eye and the stuff of every school-boy dream.

166 In sharp contrast to the light, delicate Alfa Romeos and their French and Italian counterparts, here is the solid worth of the big SSK Mercedes. About as delicate as one of Jove's thunderbolts and pretty near as quick.

166

167 The preparations for the 1930 TT in Ulster were a far cry from the excitable Italians. Officials were assisted in taking petrol samples by sizeable, if youthful, Boy Scouts. One, perched up in the background, shields the tiny viewfinder of his Kodak Box Brownie camera, extremely common in those days.

168 How is this for a relaxed atmosphere? The car is a C-Type MG Midget, but neither the place nor the owner are identified, though it looks like Donington with a faint row of pits in the background.

167

168

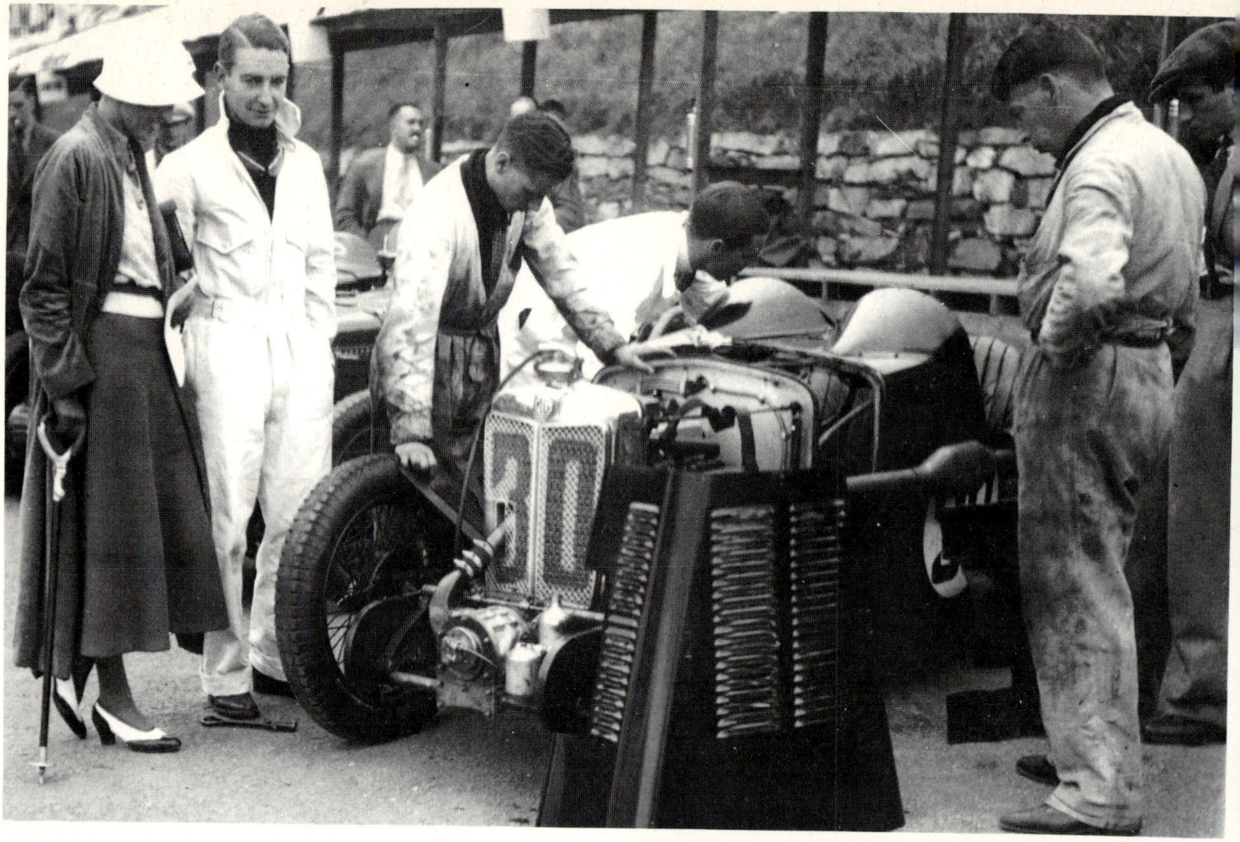

169, 170 and **171**   These are three pictures from the
1932 Ulster TT. The first two are dominated by a
now-forgotten hero in immaculate overalls who has
more of an eye for the camera than he does for the
lady. The car is a C-Type MG. In the second picture
he stands possessively by car 32, a J4 MG, but it is
not his, for it was driven in this race by Lt Col Goldie
Gardner, who is seen standing beside it in black overalls. Despite the lucky charms displayed on the
radiator, (that horse shoe should never have been the
wrong way up), this was Gardner's last road race for
it ended badly, as can be seen in the third picture.
The accident aggravated an old war-wound in his hip
and leg and he afterwards confined himself to racing
at Brooklands, and to record-breaking, for which he
became internationally famous. He set his last record
with an MG in 1952 when he was already sixty-three.
He died in 1958 after a long illness. The man in the
raincoat to the right of Gardner's car, in the second
picture, is almost certainly Cecil Kimber, the founder
and originator of the MG, who guided its fortunes
from its earliest days up to its great success in racing,
only to be brushed aside when the accountants and
take-over bids moved in.

172 As the Germans had invaded the Grand Prix scene, so they came to invade the sports cars scene a few years later. Here are the 328 BMWs lined up at Donington, being prepared with the same ruthless efficiency as the Mercedes and Auto Unions.

173 Moving on to the post-war years, efficiency has not been lost. These are the Lancias at Le Havre in 1953 before being shipped to Mexico for the Carrera.

174 A shot taken by Louis Klemantaski while
acting as passenger to Peter Collins during the Mille
Miglia. You must have had to suck pretty hard to get
the much needed drink; but in all those miles it was
probably worth it.

175 A picture taken just before the start of the
1954 Mille Miglia, which was won by Ascari. This was
an occasion when the whole town was given over to
the event.

176 Here, unusually in a sports car, is Fangio in one
of the closed Alfa Romeos developed from the 'flying
saucer'. The year is 1953, the race the Mille Miglia,
and he finished second. the number on the car also
indicates its time of departure, in this case two
minutes past six.

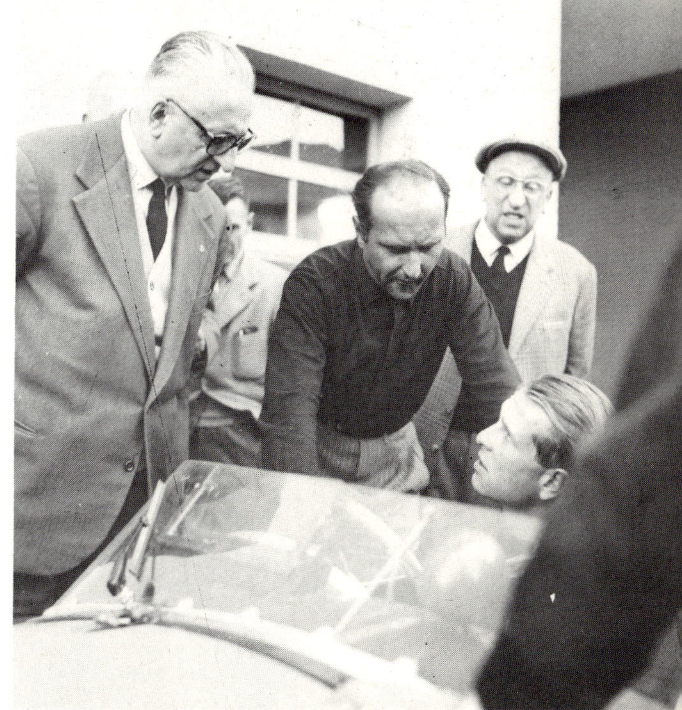

177 One of the greatest victories in the historic Mille Miglia was when Stirling Moss, on the right, drove one of the best races of his career, accompanied by Denis Jenkinson, 'Jenks' of *Motor Sport*, who wrote one of the best descriptions ever from the passenger seat. Between them the (sometimes) avuncular figure of Neubauer, the Mercedes team manager from time immemorial. The year was 1955.

178 Enzo Ferrari on the left, in glasses, talks to Peter Collins, seated in the car, while all and sundry hang onto every word. This is one of the Mille Miglia cars which Klemantski shared with Collins.

179 Waiting for the start is much the same the world over, and here is Karl Kling sitting on the sill of his Gullwing Mercedes before the start of the 1952 Carrera Panamericana in Mexico.

180 And now Le Mans. There have been so many books on this most famous of races, and so many pictures, that the best of them are all too well known. Where should one begin and how does one call a halt? Here is a small selection of photographs showing the people involved, mostly from the post-war period, but before the nature of the event moved too far away from the original idea. This shot picks up the story after the great Bentley days had passed, and the event was a tussle between Alfa Romeo and Bugatti. This is 1933 and the car in the pits is that of Nuvolari and Sommer. The cause for concern at the back of the car is a leaking petrol tank. This had been repaired constantly with chewing gum, which for some reason or other did not seem to work too well. After a while it was discovered that the mechanic who had done both the chewing and the fixing had been drinking champagne between whiles and was quite incapable of sticking the gum in the right place. At this point Nuvolari did the job himself, and was thus able to finish first at an average speed of 81·399mph, having driven more than 1,953 miles and broken all records.

181 Many years later, in 1954, it was the turn of Jaguar to head the field. Among the star partnerships of those days were Tony Rolt, on the right, and Duncan Hamilton, left, who were first in 1953 and second to Gonzales and Trintignant in a Ferrari in 1954. Although the photograph is dated 1954, the champagne makes it more likely to be 1953.

182 A line up in which almost every face belongs to someone of note, even if all will not be remembered or recognised. Among the most famous are from left to right, Reg Parnell, with hand (almost) on hip, then David Brown in dark glasses with Maurice Trintignant talking to him. Looking at the camera with his back to the racing is 'All Arms and Elbows', Innes Ireland, with Stirling Moss on his left.

183 Neither Jaguar nor Ferrari were to have it all their own way, for American millionaire and yachtsman, Briggs Cunningham, was determined to show his flag, first with modified Cadillacs and then with cars he built himself. He is seen here on the right, dressed appropriately in seafaring clothes, with Bill Aldington of Frazer-Nash fame.

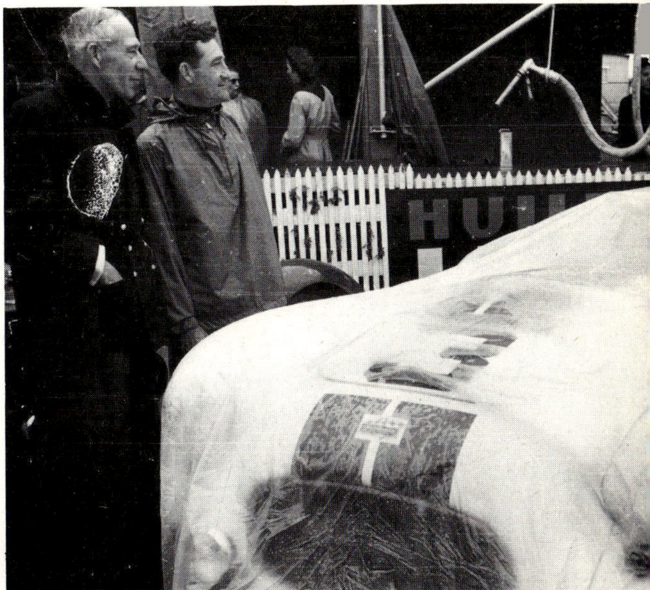

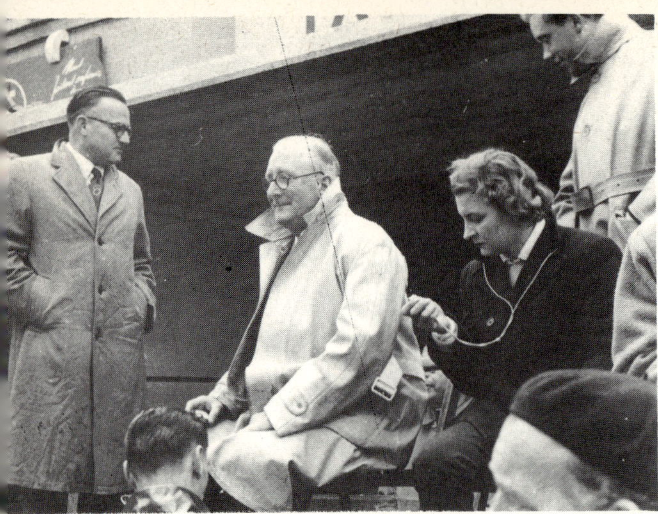

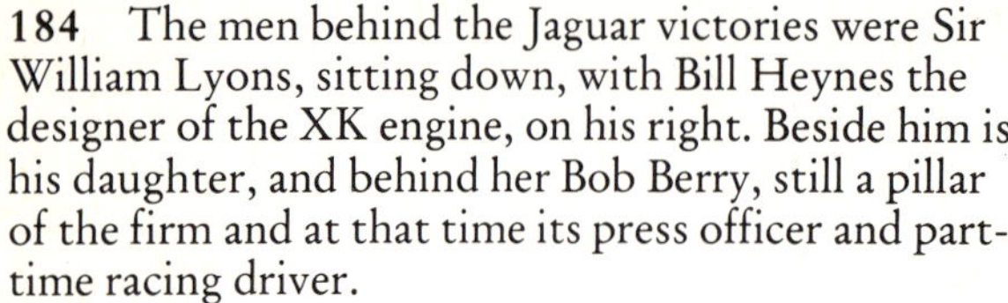

184 The men behind the Jaguar victories were Sir William Lyons, sitting down, with Bill Heynes the designer of the XK engine, on his right. Beside him is his daughter, and behind her Bob Berry, still a pillar of the firm and at that time its press officer and part-time racing driver.

185 How are the mighty fallen in the midst of battle. Catering arrangements at Le Mans being what they were, many, and even the great, decided to fend for themselves, with the attendant chores accepted in good spirit. Here, doing the somewhat primitive washing up, are, left to right, Forrest Lycett of Bentley fame, Alec Issigonis, who designed the immortal Mini, and photographer-extraordinary to the world of motor racing, Louis Klemantaski.

186 The two Mercedes cars which finished first and second in the 1952 Le Mans seen just past the Dunlop bridge, some five minutes after the start, (look at the clock if you doubt it). Their victory was tinged with sadness because for nearly all the twenty-four hours it looked to the French as if Levegh, in the French Talbot, (a thinly disguised Grand Prix car), was going to win. But Levegh had what his countrymen call a *follie de grandeur*, and was determined to drive the whole twenty-four hours by himself. He nearly did, but in his exhausted condition he overdid things and broke the crankshaft, so that Neubauer's boys, models of plan and order, swept home as victors of commonsense.

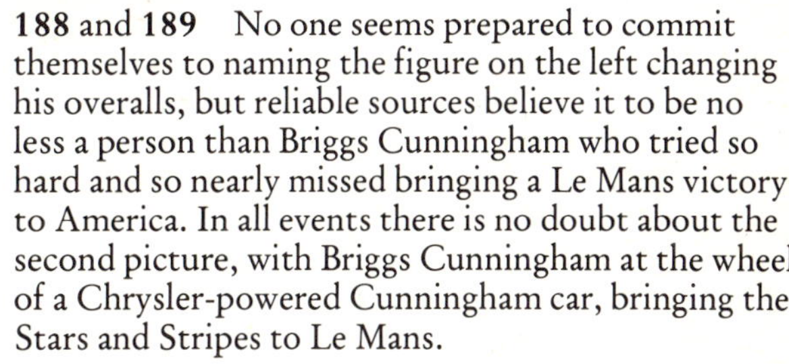

187 A return to happier thoughts the year before, when the famous duo, Whitehead and Walker, won for Jaguar. Here they are, Peter Walker sitting in the car on the left of the picture, and Peter Whitehead facing the camera on the right.

188 and 189 No one seems prepared to commit themselves to naming the figure on the left changing his overalls, but reliable sources believe it to be no less a person than Briggs Cunningham who tried so hard and so nearly missed bringing a Le Mans victory to America. In all events there is no doubt about the second picture, with Briggs Cunningham at the wheel of a Chrysler-powered Cunningham car, bringing the Stars and Stripes to Le Mans.

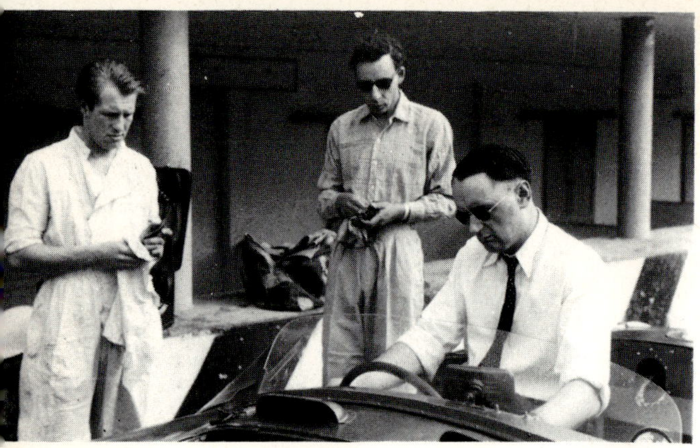

190 Perhaps the most famous Le Mans figure of them all is team manager John Wyer, seen here sitting in an Aston Martin, with George Abecassis in dark glasses, and Peter Collins. It took Aston Martin a long time to get their Le Mans victory but throughout all their struggles Wyer was in charge. He later went on to work with John Willment in the 'Mirage' set-up created by JW Automotive Engineering, to go on racing the Fords after Ford had wished to withdraw. Later, continuing their association with Gulf Oil, they moved over to Porsche in 1970. During this time Wyer was among the top team managers the world has known since the start of motor racing.

191 There is also room for some enthusiasts, even if the amateurs have had to become professional. Each year sees a spate of press handouts like this one, each with their own hopeful caption to make the news. This one reads, 'As Le Mans race day approaches, nights lengthen for the Goodrich-Greenwood Racing Team as every ounce of effort is put into the preparation of their two Chevrolet Corvettes, Group 4 Special Grand Touring Cars. Burning the midnight oil one Thursday are (centre) John Greenwood and (right) Ron Gable, discussing with Skip McCarthy, the chief engineer, the modification to dry-sump lubrication of the Corvette ZLI 7-litre engine.'

192 Here, to bring us nearer to the present, and to point the changes since the sports car was replaced by the prototype, is the 1975 Gulf car. Ford-powered with a detuned (375 hp) version of the 3-litre Grand Prix V8 engine, and driven by Derek Bell and the Belgian Jacky Ickx.

5 THE WINDS OF CHANGE

The Government health warning that motor racing forgot to heed

In the thirty years since the end of World War II, two very far reaching changes have taken place in the world of motor racing without upsetting the perenniel sameness we spoke of at the beginning of the book. The technical struggles of designs, the skill of drivers, the unflagging loyalty of mechanics, the burning of midnight oil and the high sense of endeavour, are still there, as are the faithful fans in ever increasing numbers.

But things are not what they were. From a design point of view the change from the shape of a normal private car to one in which the engine is situated between the driver and the back wheels has logic on its side; but removes the racing car even further from the cars in general use. This stems from the post-war 500cc cars which were expanded by a thoughtful few, (which included Stirling Moss), into 1,000cc models still using motor cycle engines. The small four-cylinder engines came soon after, and then the floodgates opened to everything up to a flat sixteen. It is true that Auto Union had done it all, (from the pen of Dr Porsche), before the war; but though the early 500s may have taken a hint from that, it was not much more than a hint.

The other great change was in money. From the very beginning, until about the time the engine left the front of the car, racing cars were made by motor manufacturers, the people who made ordinary road cars to sell. There were exceptions and Vanwell was one of them, but nevertheless the rule holds good. They were painted in national colours and were thought to represent their native countries in much the same way as we now see our Olympic teams doing. Red for Italy, blue for France, green for England and white (usually changed to silver) for Germany. It was clear-cut and definitive, and the rules were made by an international body called the FIA (Federation Internationale de L'Automobile), which also dealt with international touring matters. Competition was as fierce as ever and the costs were rising so oil and tyre companies came in to assist, along with the manufacturers of sparking plugs and other accessories. In return for their help they sought some kind of recognition on the car, and,

after a lot of fuss, and almost certainly not realising what they were letting themselves in for, the FIA agreed to decals, which are little notices in respect of help given, on the side of the car. The little notices became big notices and other people hopped on the band wagon. If the driver drank Bloggs Beer or used Superstar Aftershave why not put some money into the team and have a decal?

Then the flood gates opened, for in response to the idea that there was a connection between lung cancer and smoking, the cigarette manufacturers found their TV advertisements blocked. With vast sums to spend why not put the name of the product before the public on a racing car, and do not use decals, but make the whole vehicle simply look like a packet of cigarettes on wheels. Unhappily the shape of the cars was now making that more practicable, and as most of the general manufacturers had withdrawn leaving the field in the hands of specialists the transformation was complete. Sport may not quite have gone out of the window, but certainly 'showbiz' came in through the door.

This book is no place to discuss whether these changes are for better or worse; it is only necessary to record that they have taken place. On the credit side there is now vast and efficient circuit racing, not just through the European summer, but throughout the year and throughout the world. It is a huge business from which many people directly or indirectly benefit, and it has more fans and followers than ever Nuvolari knew about. On the debit side some of the fun has gone from it, for although drivers and team managers have always taken it seriously, the devil-may-care attitude that was there until the time of Mike Hawthorn and Peter Collins, who always referred to each other as 'Mon ami-mate' has been banished by the pressures of money and success. If it is true that in sport it is the game that matters and not the winning, then there is not much sport left in Grand Prix racing, or tennis, or football, or golf come to that. But this is the last quarter of the twentieth century, and as the Romans wanted their bloodthirsty circuses, so we today want this kind of Grand Prix.

193 This is perhaps the most significant picture in the book, taken at a hill climb of no great importance at Falmer, just outside Brighton, in 1948. The driver is the young Stirling Moss, and much as he came to mean to motor sport, the car is far more important. It is one of the then new Formula III 500cc cars, which were to transform the shape of the Grand Prix car itself about a decade later. The obvious comparison with the Auto Unions on previous pages cannot be denied, but in fact this was fresh thinking, and together with the ideas of Dr Porsche and Dr Rumpler before him, have led to the mid-engined Grand Prix cars of today.

194 Alberto Ascari, famous son of famous father, was the first big star to appear after the war, usually alongside his friend and mentor 'Gigi' Villoresi. Here he is in the pits and while a Talbot flashes by his mechanic anxiously tries to join together that which has come asunder. The 'SA in a Steering Wheel' sign, on the scuttle, is that of the Scuderia Ambrosiana, who raced the works Maseratis and who gave Ascari his first real chance and for whom Villoresi was already first driver.

195 One of the earliest pictures of Fangio, on the extreme left, and Gonzales in the car. The year is 1950, the place Holland on the occasion of the first Dutch Grand Prix, when both the Latin Americans drove Maseratis. Fangio had officially joined Alfa Romeo, but they had decided to give this event a miss, hence his freedom to rejoin the team sponsored by pre-war Italian-born Auto Union ace, Achille Varzi. It was around this time that someone is said to have asked Fangio if driving the way he did, even to win, was not a little dangerous; to which he is said to have replied that it was not half as dangerous as returning to the Argentine without winning! Despite the funny hat Gonzales had a wretched race as both his car and his trousers caught fire in the pits.

196 Some of the notables of the immediate post-war period in the paddock at Silverstone. Ascari is on the left in a T-shirt. The left-hand figure in the light overall is Villoresi, and beside him with goggles on his helmet is Raymond Sommer, 'The Wild Boar of the Ardennes'. Also in a white overall behind, with hand on hip, is Reg Parnell.

197 Fangio and Gonzales again, after they had both settled down and become an accepted part of the European Grand Prix scene, in spite of the papers continuing to call Gonzales 'The Wild Bull of the Pampas'. Although Fangio is seated in a Ferrari, he was not at that time driving for them, but merely trying it out for size, and looking very pleased in the process.

198 Britain's real come-back in the world of Grand Prix racing was with the Vanwall built by Tony Vandervell, the bearing manufacturer. The team was run with great efficiency by David Yorke, who is seen here examining a fractured throttle rod, which was, for a short while, an insoluble problem to the team. They eventually beat it and went on to great things until Tony Vandervell's health made him disband the stable.

199   But while Vandervell did run things they were properly run. Transporters in those days were all too often sawn-off motor coaches or just lorries. That sort of thing was not good enough for Vandervell, and his transporters were models of practicality and good advertising. As the small print on the side says, it was supplied by Leyland Motors.

200   Among the most successful of the Vanwall drivers was Tony Brooks, seen here at Monaco in 1957, after finishing a close second to Fangio, and the dust of battle still blackening his face save where his goggles have kept it clean. It was during this race that the correspondent of the *Manchester Guardian* asked the author if it was true that Brooks was a Manchester man. Feeling the answer to be 'yes', but

wanting to make sure, Vandervell was asked and replied, 'He can come from bloody Wigan for all I care, if he goes on driving like this.' A confession must also be made that the somewhat curious figure, apparently sprouting from Brooks's head, is the author trying to catch the eye of Louis Klemantaski as he took this picture.

201   This picture shows the return of Mercedes to Grand Prix racing after World War II, in the 1954 French Grand Prix, always in those days run at Rheims, with Fangio and Kling as the drivers. Fangio, on the left, won the event and while they chose to stay in the Grand Prix business, there was no beating them.

202

202 Not only did the Mercedes pre-war ideas of success stay with them, but a great many of their engineering ideas were also carried forward, such as this detachable steering wheel. This is Kling getting into his car before the race at Rheims in 1954. These streamline bodies were not a success and soon gave way to something more conventional, if less aero-dynamically satisfying.

203 As late as 1957 it was possible to have a pit stop and still win the race, indeed pit stops were still quite an ordinary part of events. Speed was essential, but not everyone managed the order that Neubauer imposed on Mercedes. Maserati at Monza, for example, did not. Somewhere buried in this melée is Fangio's Maserati. Perhaps the fact that he was number two and stopped, or was stopped, outside number four counter did not help.

203

204 Jack Brabham in one of the early Coopers. Here is the evidence of change in design, but as yet no sponsors, and no decals.

205 Here, when it was much too late, and the cars were already out of date, is a brave American attempt to break into Formula One. The scene is Monaco, the date 1960, the car a Scarab and the driver Dan Gurney. The man behind it all was Lance Reventlow, son of the Woolworth heiress, Barbara Hutton. They had some success in America with the first three front-engined sports cars that they built, but their efforts in Grands Prix were too late, though they built these front-engined Formula One cars. They appeared in the season's first three Grands Prix and then gave up. They subsequently had some success with a rear-engined sports car about 1963, but never returned to Europe.

206 The change to rear engines, and the beginnings of wealth, did at least produce some magnificent engines even in the 1½-litre days. Among the earliest efforts to develop outstanding engines were those of Coventry Climax. Better known to the older generation as the makers of fire-pump power units, the company, under the direction of Wally Hassan (right), one time Bentley mechanic and later builder of famous Brooklands cars produced, among other things, this flat-sixteen. On the left is the Chairman of Coventry Climax, Mr Lee, who had the job of finding the money!

207 Whatever engines may have been built in the past, no unit has so completely dominated the Grand Prix scene as has the V8 Cosworth, with the name of Ford on the camshaft covers. It is true that Ford signed the cheque, but the engine was the work of Keith Duckworth, seen here on the left, at the press launch in 1967 and with him are Graham Hill (centre) and Colin Chapman, whose Lotus cars were to be the first to get the unit, on the right.

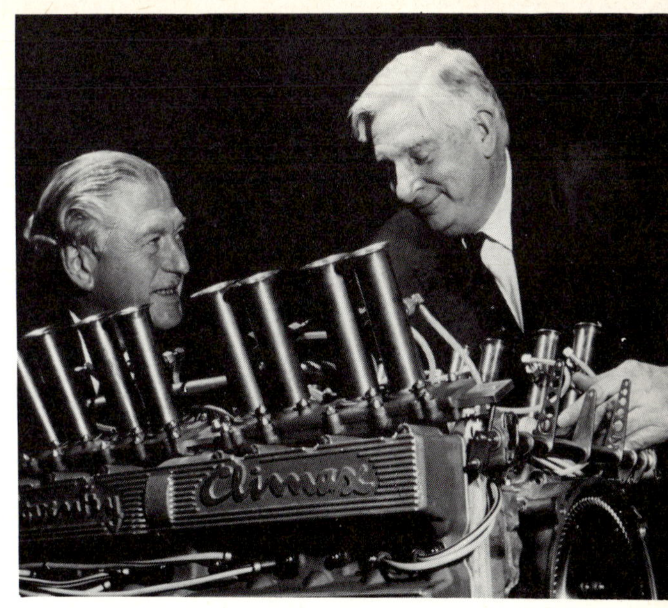

208 Throughout the first year of its use Keith Duckworth went to every event, to study its performance and talk to the men who were using it. Here he is with Graham Hill in what you might call the battle zone, in 1967.

209 The Ford Cosworth engine soon became so widely used that it was harder to find a racing car without it than with it. Fashions however still come and go and fortune smiles in different directions from year to year. All told, however, few teams have had as long a run of success as Ken Tyrell's, particularly in the Jackie Stewart days, as seen here. But to remind us that there is more to winning a Grand Prix than the driver, even if he is the one and only Jackie, here is Tyrell himself with two of his chief mechanics, Roger Hill and Roland Law.

210 This is the Maestro himself, one-time timber-merchant and now among the most successful manufacturers of racing cars, Ken Tyrell, in 1974. The picture gives a good idea of just how much racing cars now differ from the family saloon.

211 The full force and humour, (or lack of it), in the sponsorship game came in 1976 when John Surtees, with book on the right, got his sponsorship from a contraceptive company. Surtees himself won seven world championships in the motor-cycling field before turning to cars, where his career was somewhat uneven until he went to drive for Ferrari and won the Championship as well. Now a constructor, although he is not among the most successful, the publicity he provides is worth it to his sponsors. They at least had enough sense of fun to plaster London with advertisements for 'The small family car', paint their Grand Prix car as boldly as our picture shows, and leave the rest to public imagination.

212 Maybe you think this picture has somehow slipped out of place, but a closer examination will show you that it is Duckworth on the right and Colin Chapman on the left, grown a little older, with the two-hundredth Ford Cosworth engine to be delivered to Lotus; at the time cars powered by this unit had won no less than ninety-nine Grands Prix.

213 In 1969 Cosworth made one excursion into building cars themselves, and as one might expect it was controversial and experimental. It was a four-wheel-drive car, seen here being driven by Bernard Wheatcroft, who has since restored Donington Park to use as a racing circuit, and gathered together his famous collection of racing cars.

214 and **215**   Things are not always what they seem, for this might look like drivers preparing for a motor race in 1969, but in fact it is no such thing. These famous drivers had all long since retired, and the Formula Ford cars are only having a make-believe race. Someone had the idea of making a new race circuit at Jurby in the Isle of Man, and Ford provided Formula Ford cars for the assembled experts to try it out. In the first picture Moss on the right talks with Tony Brooks, who scored Great Britain's first post-war Grand Prix victory in Syracuse, and on the left Oliver Gendebien, four times winner of Le Mans. In the second picture, Moss in a Lotus number sixty-one, leads Brooks, Gendebien and Trintignant through Sandygate Corner. Nothing, sadly, seems to have come of the experiment, rather like the recent idea of having a Grand Prix round Birmingham city centre.

216   Just in case the racing world seems dominated by Grand Prix cars and that the more ordinary chaps who like to go motor racing on a Saturday afternoon are not forgotten, here for good measure are two of them, Gordon Spice on the left and Steve Neal, who race a Mini Cooper. Even here sponsorship is part of the game as the decals betray, and this one is chiefly paid for by Britax the seat-belt manufacturers.

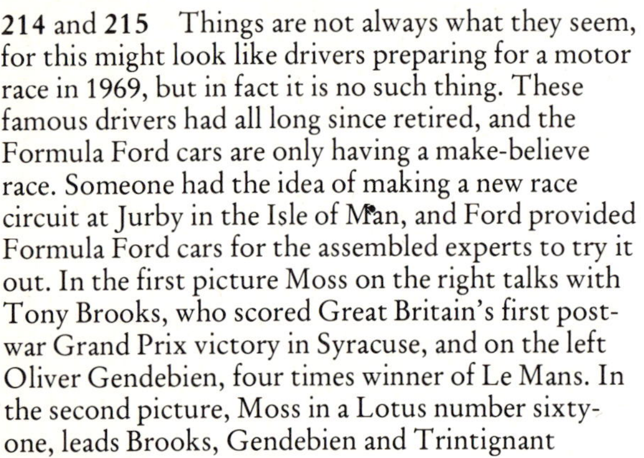

The image at the top of the page shows the Lotus team and four cars.

217

217 It is hard to know where to draw the line, but to be up to date one has to acknowledge the continuing mastery of Colin Chapman and his Lotus organisation, even if known until recently as John Player Specials. This picture gives some idea of the size of the human resources required in a Grand Prix season, and add to that the four cars and you do not need an accountant to tell you it is going to be expensive.

218 There is triumph and sadness in this picture of Chapman with the World Champion, Mario Andretti on his right and Ronnie Peterson, recently killed, on his left. But fashions change as fast as sponsors and all this may well look quite different in a year's time, and as different again a year after that, but this is what the best of Grand Prix racing looked like in 1978.

What it Takes

It would take several books to set out in real detail what happens when someone gets the idea of going into Grand Prix racing. But a recently formed team, The Arrows, makes it possible, with the following pictures, to give some idea of the size and scope of the operation. It is not all beer and skittles by any means, and even since these pictures were taken, Arrows have had their share of problems, though fortunately most of them now seem to be sorted out.

The team was put together in record time, which is not in itself important except that it demonstrates some of the exceptional skills of those concerned. The Arrows have provided a photographic coverage not often available, and the company's own announcements of intent and progress. They based their name on the initials of those most concerned: AR for Franco and Christina Ambrosio, Italians from Milan who have a personal and financial interest in the project and were instrumental in helping Riccardo Patrese to break into Formula One; R for team manager Alan Rees who was also the R in March, from which he moved to Shadows before taking his present post; O for Jackie Oliver, an experienced racing driver in his own right, and now Arrows Chief Executive (he is also ex-Shadows); W for Dave Wass, chief draughtsman and co-designer, an ex-BRM apprentice who left his original firm to join Southgate at Shadows; and finally S for Southgate himself, their Chief Designer also ex-BRM and ex-Shadows. It is clear from this that the Arrows are a splinter group of the Shadows. The Shadows claimed that the new Arrows car was too much like the previous Shadow car and they proved the point in court. However, life goes on for both the Arrows, with the re-designed car, and Shadows, and even for Riccardo Patrese who, after a brilliant drive in South Africa, annoyed the other drivers, later in the season, for being more enthusiastic than careful, but that problem too seems to have blown over. It all shows the almost desperate pressures that now attend this multi-million pound sport. There have been fusses and arguments ever since the French broke away from the then traditional races and held the first Grand Prix. But the more money there is involved, the tougher the arguments, and there has never been so much money involved as there is now.

219 The Arrows factory in the new town of Milton Keynes. Alan Rees turned the key of the door for the first time on 28 November 1977. The place was empty, the factory and offices bare. 'I didn't even have a desk, a chair, or a telephone,' Rees said. On Tuesday 29 November the telephone arrived, together with calls from all the people looking for jobs. By 5 December the machinery began to arrive.

220 With the machinery in, the mechanics began building work-benches, installing air lines, and making jigs for the team's first racing car.

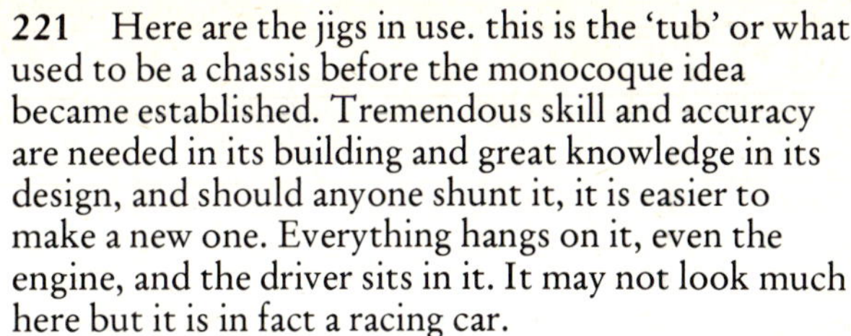

221   Here are the jigs in use. this is the 'tub' or what used to be a chassis before the monocoque idea became established. Tremendous skill and accuracy are needed in its building and great knowledge in its design, and should anyone shunt it, it is easier to make a new one. Everything hangs on it, even the engine, and the driver sits in it. It may not look much here but it is in fact a racing car.

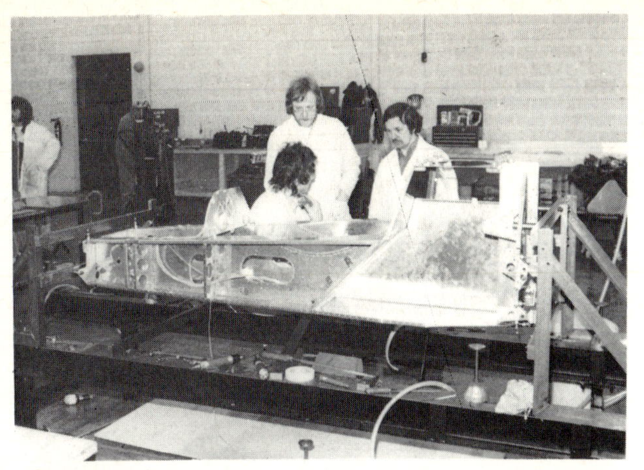

222   Patrese who is going to sit in it, stands beside it, with some of the front suspension pieces hanging on the front; the ducting is on the sides, with the engine and one of the rear hubs behind.

223   The finished article, about 19 January. The snow is a little unusual in pictures of Grand Prix cars, but the car was due to be flown to Rio two days later, and they wanted to see if it actually worked. Tony Southgate, in beret and student scarf, stands behind the car with Patrese in the driver's seat, while on the left, feeling the cold, is Alan Rees; the mechanics and the people who built the car are in the background. It is the faithful, talented few, like this, who have remained the constant factor over the years; their clothes may be different, and certainly their pay is, but the gleam in their eyes is the same as it was three-quarters of a century ago. Without it, motor racing would not exist.

36
GOODYEAR
GOODYEAR

224

RICCARDO
36
VARIG
36
GOODYEAR
GOODYEAR

225

224 From one extreme to the other. Here in Brazil they had a vital need to get the car going before official practice began, and the only available spot was a local aerodrome, although the light was fading fast.

225 This is the picture that all the pundits said would never be taken, the car on the line for the Brazilian Grand Prix, just eight weeks after they got in to the factory.

226 This picture shows an interesting contrast with pictures from the past, where team managers fought the noise to communicate with their drivers. Here, Rees talks to Patrese through the headset. One wonders how long it will be before we get back to the radio as in the Indianapolis car, and visual pit signals become a thing of the past. Careful study of the picture will show that between Brazil and South Africa there were certain changes in the paintwork, which point to a new signature on the cheques.

227 A quick stop in the South African Grand Prix, the headset plugged in, wheels being changed, and someone else on their way back into the race down the pit road.

228 After the legal fuss about the original car, here is the new one before the start of the Canadian Grand Prix. The sponsor has not changed again, it is just a change from the German Gothic lettering, (easily understood in South Africa), to something the Canadians were more readily able to assimilate.

INDEX